SUPERSTRUCTURE

The Making of the Sainsbury Centre

SUPERSTRUCTURE

The Making of the Sainsbury Centre

Edited by Jane Pavitt and Abraham Thomas

This publication accompanies the exhibition:
SUPERSTRUCTURES: The New Architecture 1960–1990
Sainsbury Centre for Visual Arts
24 March–2 September 2018

First published in Great Britain by
Sainsbury Centre for Visual Arts
Norwich Research Park
University of East Anglia
Norwich, NR4 7TJ
scva.ac.uk

British Library Cataloguing-in-Publication Data.
A catalogue record is available from the British Library.

ISBN 978 0946 009732

Exhibition Curators: Jane Pavitt and Abraham Thomas
Book Design: Johnson Design
Book Project Editor: Rachel Giles
Project Curator: Monserrat Pis Marcos
Printed and bound in the UK by Pureprint Group

First edition

10 9 8 7 6 5 4 3 2 1

Unless otherwise stated, all dates of built projects refer to their date of completion.

Building credits run in the order of architect followed by structural engineer.

SAINSBURY CENTRE 40 YEARS 1978–2018

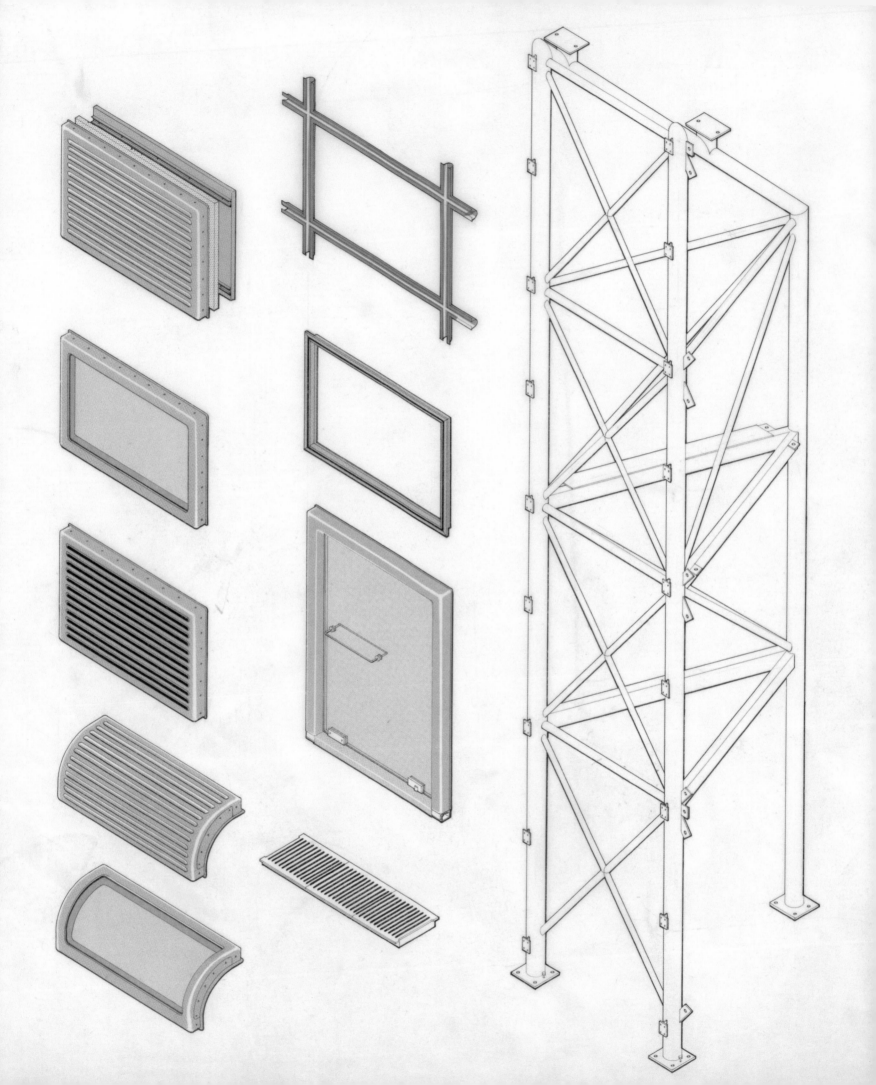

Contents

D.2074

Roof Plan.

a bit more graphic.

D.688

Foreword **David Sainsbury**

When my father decided to give his collection to the University of East Anglia and a building to house it, he could have chosen a famous and established architect to build it. But instead he went and quietly looked at the work of a number of architects, and eventually chose Norman Foster, who was then largely unknown, on the simple basis that he found his buildings exciting and beautiful.

This was typical of the way my parents built up their collection. They were totally uninterested in what other people and the critics thought, and bought only the work of artists they found beautiful and exciting.

This approach to art collecting resulted in them buying the work of three of the greatest artists of the twentieth century when they were unknown: Henry Moore, Francis Bacon and Alberto Giacometti. They also bought many world art objects at a time when they were largely unappreciated.

It was also very typical of my parents that having chosen Norman they worked very closely with him on the brief for the building. As a result, 'The Living Area' is modelled on the way they showed objects and pictures in their Georgian house in London, as that is the way they thought works of art should be seen.

At the same time, they gave Norman the artistic space to develop his ideas, and to create a building which, technologically and aesthetically, played a key role in opening up a new frontier in British architecture. It was also a building that my parents and I loved from day one, and my father always used to say that it was the best object in his collection.

SUPERSTRUCTURES
THE NEW ARCHITECTURE
1960–1990

Jane Pavitt and Abraham Thomas

Introduction

'It may well be that what we have hitherto understood as architecture, and what we are beginning to understand of technology are incompatible disciplines.
The architect who proposes to run with technology knows now he will be in fast company, and that, in order to keep up, he may have to emulate the Futurists and discard his whole cultural load, including the professional garments by which he is recognised as an architect.'[1]

Reyner Banham, 1960

In 1960, the Norwich-born architectural critic Peter Reyner Banham concluded his pioneering study of the Modern Movement, *Theory and Design in the First Machine Age*, with a call to arms. On the cusp of a 'second machine age', with rapid advances in manufacturing, engineering and mechanical services, the future of architecture lay in proper engagement with the 'mind of technology'. In his view the architecture of the International Style had failed to deliver on the promises of the first machine age, limited by aesthetic and formal concerns. Here, then, was a second chance.

Nearly thirty years later, at the time of his death in 1988, Banham was engaged in a project to 'define, chronicle and understand' an 'alternative modernism' which had by then become known as High Tech.[2] The label referred to the marriage of engineering and architecture, as practised by a generation of (largely) British architects. The names most frequently associated with this approach were the quartet of Norman Foster, Richard Rogers, Nicholas Grimshaw and Michael Hopkins, who rose to international prominence in the 1970s and 1980s. Their practice was rooted in the utopian ideas of the Modern Movement and the engineering advances of the nineteenth and twentieth centuries. The conditions of post-war architecture and industry shaped their ideas. Their experiments in the late 1960s and early 1970s were inspired by innovations in prefabrication and system building techniques, many of them from the US, and were also infused with the spirit of 1960s technological utopianism, which dreamt of mechanised, adaptive environments for future forms of living and working. In the 1970s and 1980s, their names were associated with high-profile commissions for museums and exhibition spaces, factories and office buildings. Later in their careers, building for transport, including airports and rail stations, also became a feature of their work.

Their buildings, whilst individually distinct, were thought by Banham to adhere to three stylistic principles of 'structure, services and colour'. Whether a simple industrial 'shed' or a high-rise office complex, what these buildings had in common were exposed steel structures, open and flexible interiors, 'zoned' services and as much off-site construction as possible. Structure and services were often, but not always, expressed with a vibrant use of colour. As Banham points out, these buildings were not only structural envelopes but also 'complete and active environmental systems'.

The Sainsbury Centre for Visual Arts is one of the most outstanding examples of this approach to architecture. Its opening in 1978 was held up as evidence that British architects led the field in advanced engineering, as American architect Philip Johnson playfully observed: 'There isn't anyone in America who can do something as good as the Sainsbury Centre. England has at once become the leader in the engineering and technology game.'[3] The late 1970s was indeed a high point in British architecture: the Centre Pompidou in Paris, by Richard Rogers and Renzo Piano, had been completed a year earlier, as had the critically acclaimed steel and glass Hopkins House, designed by Michael and Patty Hopkins for their family in Hampstead, London. All of these architects were closely associated with each other; Foster and Rogers worked in practice together from 1963–8; Hopkins worked in partnership with Foster before setting up in practice with his wife, Patty, in 1976. Their firms became synonymous with High Tech, although individually they have distanced themselves from that term. Their work is part of a long tradition of Modernism and engineering innovation, explored in this essay, which has had a profound influence on the shape of our buildings and cities.

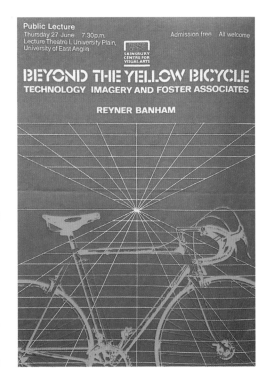

Right. Poster announcing lecture by Reyner Banham, 'Beyond the Yellow Bicycle', (c.1985), artist unknown.

Far right. Sainsbury Centre for Visual Arts Crescent Wing extension Norwich, UK, 1991 Foster Associates/ Anthony Hunt Associates

Above. Centre Georges
Pompidou
Paris, France, 1977
Piano + Rogers/
Ove Arup & Partners

Left. Hopkins House
London, UK, 1977
Hopkins Architects/
Anthony Hunt Associates

The making of the Sainsbury Centre

Commissioned in 1974 and opened in 1978, the Sainsbury Centre was built to house the donation of Robert and Lisa Sainsbury's collection to the University of East Anglia. Norman Foster, despite having no experience in museum design, was selected as architect by Robert Sainsbury on the strength of a complex of buildings built for the Norwegian Shipping Line Fred Olsen (Fred Olsen Amenity Building and Passenger Terminal, 1968–70). Sainsbury admired Foster's unconventional solution to the complexity of functions required by the company and the lightweight steel and glass structure used. The first meeting between Foster and the Sainsburys – at their house in Smith Square, London – was a meeting of like minds. The Sainsburys gave their architect a surprisingly open brief: 'Architecturally, Norman Foster was given only two guidelines, we did *not* want a monument to ourselves or to him, and we *did* want a positive statement.'[4]

The commission was for a public museum for the collection with a restaurant; and accommodation for the University's School of Arts. It was assumed there would need to be at least two buildings. However, early on, Foster arrived at the idea for a single building incorporating everything, on the edge of the University campus and orientated towards the lake.

At first, Foster was engaged as the architect of the building, working with Dutch designer Kho Liang le, who was responsible for the interiors. Kho had been friends with the Sainsburys since the 1960s, designing exhibitions for their collection, and so had close knowledge of their expectations for the display of objects. Tragically, his involvement in the project was to be short-lived due to his untimely death from cancer in 1975. Rather than engage another interior designer, it was decided that Foster would assume responsibility for the whole project. Nevertheless, the building is a true product of collaboration – the Sainsburys were intimately involved in the design process and decision making; the structural engineer Anthony Hunt, who had worked with Foster since the mid-1960s, was charged with realising the complex structure; American lighting consultant Claude Engel and designer George Sexton were brought in to develop the building's innovative lighting effects. The team at Foster Associates included Loren Butt, Roy Fleetwood, Birkin Haward, Richard Horden and Ian Ritchie.

Foster's proposition was for a single-span structure 150 metres (492 feet) in length – an extruded steel portal frame with interchangeable cladding panels made from glass or aluminium. The enormous and adaptable interior space is achieved by the double-skinned construction, which provides a void between inner and outer skin in which the services are located (such as kitchens and bathrooms), in addition to the serviced basement 'spine'. The building's lighting is controlled by motorised louvres with reflective surfaces and perforated slats. Intermittent glazed roof panels provide natural light; the ceiling spotlights are serviced and adjusted from within the double-skinned void, saving the need for ladders or scaffold. Foster called this 'tuning the building'.[5]

As Jonathan Glancey explains later in this book, Foster's Sainsbury Centre is indebted both to his lifelong fascination with aircraft (he describes the Boeing 747-400 as the 'ultimate technological building-site') and also to his early exposure to system building methods in the United States. His approach drew him to work with others who saw the potential for architecture's reinvention:

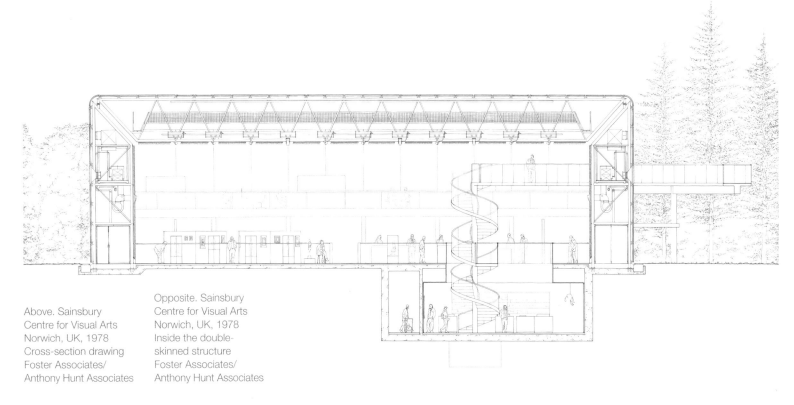

Above. Sainsbury
Centre for Visual Arts
Norwich, UK, 1978
Cross-section drawing
Foster Associates/
Anthony Hunt Associates

Opposite. Sainsbury
Centre for Visual Arts
Norwich, UK, 1978
Inside the double-
skinned structure
Foster Associates/
Anthony Hunt Associates

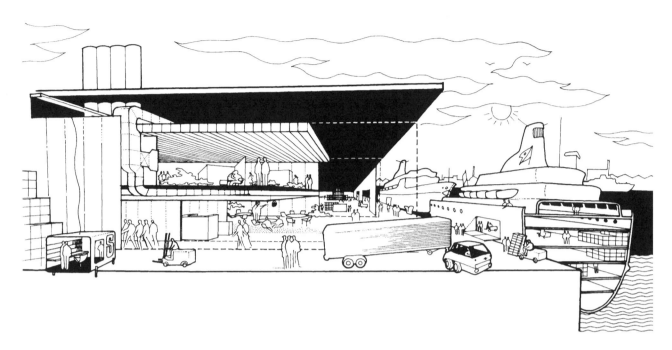

Left. Fred Olsen Amenity
Building
London, UK, 1970
Demolished 1988
Cross-sectional
perspective drawing
Foster Associates/
Anthony Hunt Associates

Below. Biosphere
Environment Museum
Montreal, Canada, 1967
Richard Buckminster
Fuller, Fuller & Sadao
Originally built as the USA
Pavilion for Expo '67.

In 1976, a fire destroyed
the acrylic cladding,
although the hard
steel truss survived.
The dome was rebuilt
and opened as a
museum in 1995.

not only the architects with whom he collaborated (from the early Team 4 partnership with Wendy Foster and Richard and Su Rogers, to Foster + Partners' global community of around 1500 staff today), but also engineers like Hunt; and clients open to new ideas, like the Sainsburys. Perhaps one of the most inspiring relationships of Foster's career was with the legendary American engineer-architect Richard Buckminster Fuller. Fuller's visionary approach to prefabrication (the 'Dymaxion House' concept) and lightweight engineering (the geodesic dome) had been profoundly influential on architects' training in the 1960s.

A simple measure of Fuller's approach can be found in his 'requirement' that 'any draughtsmen or any architectural students should always have the weights of (their) materials.'[6] 'How much does your building weigh, Mr Foster?' Fuller asked Foster of the Sainsbury Centre. Foster, an exemplary 'student' of Fuller, supplied the answer: 5,618.6 tons. Not only that, but the building's 'superstructure' – its steel skeleton, aluminium cladding, sub-frame, mechanical and electrical equipment, glazing, louvres and interior fittings (stairs, walkways, partitions and so forth) amounted to around only one-fifth of that total weight. The remaining four-fifths (4,507 tons) was the weight of the building's concrete substructure. Compare that to Fuller's own calculation of the weight of the dome of St Peter's Cathedral in Rome: 30,000 tons, or the same weight as the QE2. Foster's building clearly met the Fuller test.

The Sainsbury Centre provoked a storm of debate in architectural circles when it opened in 1978. Praised for its technical ingenuity and the quality of its material construction, critics were divided over its disciplined, functional appearance. Traditionalists argued that the visual language of the 'shed' or the 'aircraft hangar' was inappropriate for a museum of art; Postmodernists rejected the building's extreme Modernism in an era of contextual complexity and pluralism. Others situated it within a tradition of British invention which ranged from the Nissen Hut to the Crystal Palace. The building epitomised a new architecture born of this technological spirit: a 'well-serviced shed' with a lightweight and extendable steel structure wrapped in a 'skin' of glass and plastic clip-on panels; adaptable (and adapted) as the building's functions changed or grew over time. In 1991, the building was extended to provide additional office, exhibition and collections space. The Crescent Wing extends the building underground towards the lake, emerging in a crescent of glass and steel.

40 years after its completion, the Sainsbury Centre still has the capacity to surprise and delight, as well as challenge expectations. Part of this is the drama of its site: encountered on arrival by car or by foot through the concrete megastructure of Denys Lasdun's 1960s university campus, or glimpsed through the bucolic setting of the English landscape. The building hovers as if in temporary flight suspension, unweathered and gleaming (due to its replacement

cladding, although this was never a building designed to gain the patina of age), declaring its modernity in steel and glass, despite these materials having long since become part of a familiar heritage of modern Britain. Once inside, admiration for its technical virtuosity gives way to more aesthetic consideration of its spatial and lighting effects. The architect Charles Jencks observed:

We suspend our disbelief, as we do before art, to judge it on its own terms; and these terms are, once again, extreme. The light quality of the ceiling is unlike anything we've ever seen before at this scale – shimmering, playful, iridescent, disturbing, like a thousand Bridget Riley optical vibrations laid end to end. It goes on buzzing and dancing overhead, with its motorised louvres, not for a hundred feet, but for over four hundred.[7]

Sainsbury Centre for Visual Arts
Norwich, UK 1978
Interior view of collections display
Foster Associates/
Anthony Hunt Associates

The idea of High Tech

The new architecture only acquired its contentious label of 'High Tech' in the late 1970s. Like many stylistic terms given to architectural developments, it has largely been rejected by those architects it describes. For those who adhered to a Modernist tradition and stood in opposition to Postmodern ideas of contextualism, ornament and historicism, the idea of style as decoration was anathema. For those associated with the technological strain of the new architecture, the emphasis was on what could be achieved through material and engineering solutions. It was often a case of employing the most appropriate technology for a project, finding solutions sometimes in 'at hand' or 'off-the-shelf' materials and technologies, or borrowing from industries outside of architecture, such as aircraft and car manufacture. The point of 'tech' – whether high or low – was to do to building what had been achieved in industries that had advanced considerably under post-war conditions. This is not to say that it was not visionary, nor concerned with aesthetic effect. Banham offered a simple definition in 1988 – 'the most recent way of bringing advanced engineering within the discipline of architecture, comparable with the achievements of Peter Behrens and Auguste Perret in the first fifteen years of the present [twentieth] century.'[8] This definition had the advantage of describing a *method* rather than a *style*, and of situating it within the canonical roots of early Modernism.

In fact, the term had been popularised in a 1978 interior design book entitled *High-Tech: The Industrial Style and Source Book for the Home* by US journalists Joan Kron and Suzanne Slesin, which placed less emphasis on contemporary architectural practice, focusing instead on a DIY 'industrial chic' for modern decor, achieved by shopping at hardware stores. Kron and Slesin's book had more in common with the industrial salvage movement of the late 70s and early 80s; the Postmodern styling of shop and nightclub interiors, and fashion for 'loft living' than it did with the architecture of Foster, Rogers et al. However, in an article in 1983 in *Architectural Review*, entitled 'High-Tech: Another British Thoroughbred', the critic Peter Buchanan situated this architectural tendency in a chronology of British engineering inventiveness, linking the nineteenth-century 'cast-iron prefabricated component construction' of glass houses and railway sheds with a boyish fascination with 'machines and their performance, particularly with cars, trains and aeroplanes', Meccano sets and the 'explanatory cut-aways of modern machinery' found in the pages of the *Eagle* comic.[9]

Notwithstanding the arguments of the architects who continue to see the application of the term 'High Tech' as reductive, the label has stuck. Architectural writer Charles Jencks identifies the Foster/ Rogers tendency, in buildings such as the Sainsbury Centre and Pompidou, as 'late Modern' in that 'it is still committed to the tradition of the new, and does not have a complex relationship to the past.'[10] The latter part of the statement is easily disputed when considering the emphasis that, say, Foster and Hopkins have placed on their early interest in traditional architecture and in making measured drawings of timber-frame construction, for example. Nor does it acknowledge the ways in which, say, Foster's Willis Faber & Dumas Building (Ipswich, 1975) or Rogers' Lloyd's of London (1978–86) are in dialogue with their historic urban settings. But their interest in the past was certainly at odds with the prevailing Postmodern 'complex' concerns for pluralism, revivalism and stylistic quotation.

So, in effect, High Tech is an inadequate yet usefully succinct term to describe a persistent technological Modernism which surfaced in the 1960s, laid claim to a grand engineering tradition, and produced a series of buildings which, whilst individually distinct, shared a common approach to services, structures, assembly, materials and construction methods. It is also a term which many people associate more with racing cars and computers than they do with architecture. Notwithstanding this, in this essay we use it as shorthand and in Banham's way, to describe an ethos rather than a style, and in the knowledge that a 'serviced building' for the twenty-first century now incorporates the kind of smart technologies and products that the 1960s experimentalists could only dream of.

Three early projects

Three early projects encapsulate the idea of an 'engineering-advanced architecture' and exemplified Banham's call for architects to 'run with technology'. They also marked the genesis of the ideas and partnerships that would distinguish High Tech. Their methods of design and construction were experimental, using untested techniques for innovative solutions: the Reliance Controls Electronics Factory in Swindon, Wiltshire (1967) by Team 4 (the practice comprised of Norman and Wendy Foster, and Richard and Su Rogers); the Rogers' Zip-Up House Prototype of 1968 (both projects with engineer Anthony Hunt); and the Student Hostel Service Tower in Paddington, London, designed by Nicholas Grimshaw in partnership with Terry Farrell (also 1967).

Foster and Rogers had met whilst at Yale University in 1961, both the recipients of coveted scholarships. They were from markedly different backgrounds. Foster grew up in Manchester, attended grammar school and studied architecture at Manchester University after completing national service. Rogers, born into a wealthy Anglo-Italian family and whose uncle was the renowned architect and editor Ernesto Rogers, studied at the Architectural Association in London. He was attending Yale with his wife Su, who was studying urban planning. At Yale, Foster and Rogers became close due to shared projects and interests, under, most notably, the presiding influence of Louis Kahn and the tutelage of Serge Chermayeff. Another visiting architect from England, James Stirling, arrived to teach a semester and quickly bonded with the English students. After completing their

study there, they gained experience in various offices (Foster with Yale director Paul Rudolph, and then as a research fellow with Chermayeff, and Rogers with Skidmore, Owings & Merrill) and also travelled further afield. Richard and Su Rogers, for example, toured the buildings of Frank Lloyd Wright. Both Foster and Rogers visited California, where they were influenced by the steel and glass architecture of the Case Study Houses (notably designed by Charles and Ray Eames and Craig Ellwood) and the prefabricated, serviced and modular prototype of the School Construction Systems Development (SCSD) project, designed by Ezra Ehrenkrantz (1962). Returning home, Rogers suggested they set up in practice. Team 4 was founded in 1963 by Su Rogers, Georgie Cheesman, Norman Foster and Richard Rogers. Cheesman withdrew from the partnership early on and was replaced by her sister Wendy who was at that point part way through her architectural training. Wendy and Norman later married and Team 4 became a partnership of two couples for its short existence. Team 4's first commission, Creek Vean (1964–7), was a house for Su Rogers' parents, Marcus and Rene Brumwell, in Cornwall. The house, reminiscent of Frank Lloyd Wright in its organic relationship to its landscape, brought the team their first challenge in working with the 'conservative outlook of the building trades' and spurred them further in the direction of prefabrication and factory-made components. One notable innovation at Creek Vean was the use of Neoprene gasket joints for glazing (an innovation borrowed from the car industry and one of the construction methods closely

Left. Creek Vean House
Feock, UK, 1966
Interior view
Team 4/
Anthony Hunt Associates

Below. The Cockpit,
Creek Vean House
Feock, UK, 1966

associated with later High Tech). During the development of the project, Team 4 also created a tiny retreat for their clients, buried in the earth with a glass 'hood' like the cockpit of an aeroplane, giving a view of the creek beyond (The Cockpit at Creek Vean House, 1963).

The commission for the Reliance Controls Factory came from a recommendation by James Stirling, who had been approached to design the building but found the project too small for his practice. Stirling was busy with the design of the University of Cambridge's History Faculty Building (1963–8) at the time, and so suggested his former students from Yale. Reliance Controls was a testbed opportunity for the young partnership. It was one of the first industrial facilities in the UK to combine the needs of factory, office and research station in a single brief. Their solution was a steel frame structure designed to be extendable and with a completely flexible interior, which exemplified the idea of the 'well-serviced shed'. Services were contained within a core under the floorplate of the building, leaving the structure open and suited to future adaptation. The steel frame was visibly expressed, with steel sheet cladding set within the frame rather

than on top of it, and a system of cross-bracing which extended all around the building. The cross-bracing was not strictly functional, but gave the building its distinctive aesthetic and became a trademark of later High Tech buildings. In the words of Richard Rogers, 'Reliance was a breakthrough. We had found our style'.[11]

Reliance Controls set the pace for a distinctively new approach to architecture. First, it was a true collaboration between its architects and engineer, Anthony Hunt (although the aesthetic treatment of the cross-bracing gave him a moment of disquiet, as it went beyond the purely functional). Secondly, it was a building type for a new age of advanced electronics industry demanding a 'clean' factory environment. Thirdly, it was organised according to an anti-hierarchical idea of the workplace where managers, office and factory workers occupied the same space. Reliance Controls employed lessons from American architecture observed by Rogers and Foster on their extended study visits in the early 1960s: the 'kit of parts' assembly methods employed by Charles and Ray Eames, and the prototype of the School Construction Systems Development (SCSD)

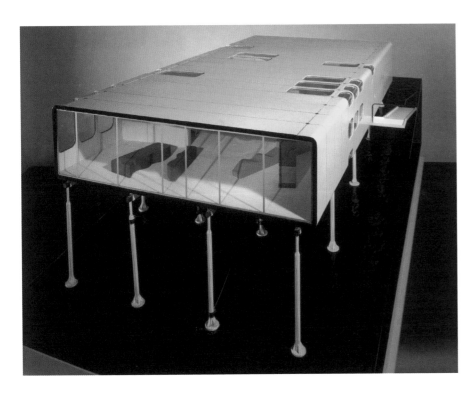

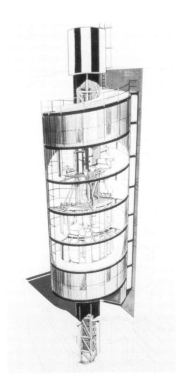

Left. Practice
Model of the 'Zip-Up'
House (unbuilt), 1968
Acrylic
Richard + Su Rogers/
Anthony Hunt
Associates

Right. Drawing for
Service Tower for
Student Housing
London, UK, 1967
Farrell/Grimshaw
Partnership/
Ove Arup & Partners

Opposite. Reliance
Controls Factory
Swindon, UK, 1965–6
Demolished 1991
Detail of cross-bracing
Team 4/
Anthony Hunt
Associates

project, designed by Ezra Ehrenkrantz, described later in this essay. The factory won the 1967 Financial Times Industrial Building of the Year award.

Reliance Controls was to be Team 4's last project together. The two couples went their separate ways into new partnerships. Richard + Su Rogers (as their practice was known) sustained themselves with private commissions: a roof-top building extension to the headquarters of the Design Research Unit, run by Marcus Brumwell (1969–71); a house for the artist and photographer Humphrey Spender (1967–8) and for Richard's parents in Wimbledon, London (1968–9). Both houses were viewed as prototypes for mass production, but in effect were highly bespoke. The Zip-Up prototype, by comparison, was the Rogers' model of the factory-made house, designed for a competition for 'The House of Today' for the 1969 Ideal Home Exhibition. The competition was sponsored by the chemical company DuPont, who were behind the development of many polymers which came to be used in construction, including Neoprene and Teflon. Of monocoque construction (a nod to the car industry), the system employed aluminium-skinned panels with a cellular PVC core (used in aircraft design). The panels were assembled into 'rings' which slotted together into an extendable tube with no need for internal support or subdivision, 'zipped' together with Neoprene gaskets. Mounted onto steel jacks which could be adjusted to suit different terrain, the houses were intended to simply plug into existing services. Phase 2 (1971) developed a two-storey version; another (the Universal Oil Products (UOP) factory concept (1969), 'grew' the idea for industrial-scale application, with the addition of a steel frame (a version of which was eventually built for UOP in 1973–4,

by Piano + Rogers). The Zip-Up method demonstrated the Rogers' thinking that buildings could be designed as ready-made 'products'. The striking use of colour also served to further distance the buildings from conventional material-use and fabrication methods.

This principle of building-as-product was also explored in the design of the Student Hostel Service Tower, by Nicholas Grimshaw and Terry Farrell, a commission to convert six London nineteenth-century terraced houses into a hostel for university students. It was their first project. Their solution was a circular tower with a helical ramp housing 35 prefabricated plastic bathroom 'capsules' and laundry facilities (made from glass-reinforced polyester or GRP), suspended from a central steel mast (rather like Fuller's mast-hung Dymaxion House, which had been conceived in the 1920s but not built until 1945). The idea was that students could access the bathroom tower from any floor, traversing the ramp until they found a free cubicle. The steel mast also served to support the crane which levered the bathrooms into position on the constrained site. The project was indebted to the ideas of the experimental group Archigram (Grimshaw had been taught by Peter Cook, one of the group's key members, at the Architectural Association), and Buckminster Fuller, whose advocacy of lightweight materials and prefabrication had been inspirational to a young generation of students at the AA, and who Grimshaw saw as 'a kind of idol'. Indeed, Fuller's visit to the Service Tower in 1967 conferred approval on the project. At the time, the Service Tower was the built project that came closest to what Banham had described as a 'clip-on architecture'[12] – Grimshaw has described it as 'a cross between mechanical engineering, sculpture and rocket science.'[13]

The engineering tradition

The serviced shed, the plastic house, the plug-in module, the extendable building, 'dry' construction: all of these ideas were in wide circulation throughout the 1960s, through the pages of experimental and technical journals, in lectures and student discussions. American ideas dominated, and the close degree of exchange between the UK and the USA fuelled this interest: Buckminster Fuller visited the UK on frequent lecture visits; his ideas were extolled by critics (Banham) and influential figures such as Cedric Price, who was also enthusiastic about the technological advances of the US military, ranging from pneumatic structures to cybernetic command-and-control systems. For those who had the opportunity (like Foster and Rogers), study visits to the US were the most crucial educative process, but some British architectural schools, such as the AA (where Price taught) and the Regent Street Polytechnic (now the University of Westminster) also provided exposure to these ideas. Student projects from the mid-1960s give an inkling of the preoccupations that would emerge: Andrew Holmes, for example, who later worked with Rogers and Renzo Piano on the Centre Pompidou, and Rogers' Inmos and Patmos projects, designed a prefabricated steel housing system called 'Flexikit' (1967). Nicholas Grimshaw's MA thesis was a proposal for an 'urban university' clearly influenced by Archigram, Price, and cybernetics guru Gordon Pask, and featured the service tower idea that he would use for the Paddington students' hostel in 1967.

Student projects such as these were frequently published in the pages of *Archigram* (1961–74), the eponymous magazine produced by the collective comprised of Warren Chalk, Peter Cook, Dennis Crompton, David Greene, Ron Herron and Mike Webb. *Archigram* was a bridge between the tradition of British invention, its engineering heritage, and the futurological excitement of the 60s. The magazine mixed a fascination with the 'grand' engineering tradition of Brunel, Paxton and Eiffel, the post-war experimentalism of Fuller, designer Jean Prouvé and engineer Konrad Wachsmann and the 'technological frontiers' of new electronics, cybernetics, chemicals and bioengineering. Combining this with a science-fiction romanticism and a Pop sensibility, the magazine created what Simon Sadler has described as 'inventories of the future-at-hand'.[14] Whereas Archigram's own architectural projections remained largely in the

AERIAL VIEW FESTIVAL SITE   South Bank Exhibition   Festival of Britain 1951

Above. Aerial view of the Festival of Britain site, showing the Dome of Discovery. London, UK, 1951

Right. The Crystal Palace being reconstructed at Sydenham London, UK, 1854 Originally constructed 1851, rebuilt 1854, destroyed 1936 Joseph Paxton/ William Cubitt (engineer), Fox, Henderson & Co. (building contractors)

Forth Bridge
Firth of Forth, UK, 1889
John Fowler and
Benjamin Baker

realm of unbuilt or unbuildable, their ideas filtered through to the generation of architects who became involved in High Tech.

So why did such an approach take root in Britain in the 1960s? The idea of the technocratic society was given rhetorical impetus by prime minister Harold Wilson's famous 1963 speech in which he referred to the 'white heat' of technological revolution.[15] A post-war fascination with the 'heroism' of invention (from the Spitfire to *Dan Dare*) was notable. Victorian ingenuity was celebrated in national projections such as the 1951 Festival of Britain; but in other respects its industrial and engineering heritage was under threat from the sweeping pace of 'modernisation' (such as the closing of numerous railway branch lines and stations as part of the Beeching cuts of the 1960s). Perhaps what drew attention to this grand tradition was not only the beauty and ingenuity of threatened engineering structures.[16] It was also the opportunity to lay claim to its legacy.

Take, for example, the Iron Bridge in Coalbrookdale, Shropshire, designed by Thomas Pritchard (1779). The bridge was the first significant structure to use the modern material of cast iron and became a worldwide symbol for Britain's Industrial Revolution. Anticipating the aesthetic possibilities of industrial materials that would be fully exploited during the twentieth century, the bridge's sinuous curves and geometric harmonies proved that decorative complexity and structural integrity could be combined with a deft

touch. In the next century, the dawn of the railway age generated the need not only for more ambitious bridges, but also for long-span train sheds to service new terminus buildings across the country. Iconic projects such as Scotland's Forth Bridge (1889) with its soaring 'pure structure' steel spans and unadorned engineering components, or Isambard Kingdom Brunel's cathedral-like Paddington station (1854) with its vaulted open-plan arrangement, exemplified the structural legibility and inventive construction methods that were possible with these new materials. The 1950s and 1960s saw a new engagement with the work of these engineers: biographies of Brunel and another engineer of early iron structures, Thomas Telford, were published, and heritage societies dedicated to industrial archaeology founded.[17]

Arguably, the building with the most impact during this period of technological innovation was Joseph Paxton's Crystal Palace, built for London's Great Exhibition of 1851. The Exhibition's Royal Commissioners had already rejected a number of other submissions and were fast running out of time. Paxton's proposal for a simple framed building using dry construction and prefabricated cast-iron, glass and timber elements meant it could be constructed relatively quickly, and his design was approved immediately. The structure incorporated many of the principles of later High-Tech buildings: a flexible modular plan, lightweight materials, standardised prefabricated components, structural clarity and rapid site assembly.[18]

The demountability and extendability of the Crystal Palace became crucial a few years later when it was dismantled, enlarged and relocated to Sydenham in south London, where it was to remain as a permanent structure until destroyed by fire in 1936.

Ian Ritchie's Messe-Leipzig Glass Hall (1992–6) is perhaps the most obvious progeny of the Crystal Palace, given its function as a giant trade exhibition hall. The hall (conceived by gmp architects, Hannover, who invited Ritchie to collaborate with IPP Ingenieurbüro and HL-Technik on the project) is 244 metres (800 feet) long, 80 metres (262 feet) wide and provides 350,000 square metres (3.8 million square feet) of space. Its immense span is facilitated by tubular steel arches, positioned at 25-metre (82-foot) intervals, which support a glazed steel lattice structure.

The legacy of the nineteenth-century modular, extruded shed is also reflected in buildings such as the Sainsbury Centre and Rogers' Inmos Microprocessor Factory (1982–7) – projects conceived with flexibility of function and scalability in mind. The Inmos Factory continues a tradition of earlier factory structures that became influential not only because of functional adaptability and material innovation, but also because of their visual metaphors of mass-industrialisation and efficient production processes. Another industrial forebear in the vein of Brunel and Paxton was Owen Williams' factory for Boots in Beeston, Nottinghamshire (1932), which boasted a reinforced concrete structural frame that could incorporate a seemingly uninterrupted envelope of glass panels, anticipating the curved, glazed skin and internal flexibility of Foster Associates' Willis Faber & Dumas building over forty years later. In the United States, Albert Kahn was designing breathtakingly expansive steel-framed and glazed car factories for Ford and Packard during the early decades of

the twentieth century. In 1927, Ford commissioned Charles Sheeler to produce a series of publicity photographs depicting the vast scale of production at their River Rouge plant, just outside Detroit. Resembling the disorientating networks of walkways and staircases of Piranesi's etchings of imaginary prisons, Sheeler's compositions of criss-crossed conveyors, steel girders and towering smoke stacks provided compelling imagery of a technological Utopia. Images by Sheeler and other artists inspired by modern machinery and production, such as Diego Rivera and Fernand Léger, and events such as Philip Johnson's influential Machine Art exhibition at the Museum of Modern Art in 1934, all contributed to a new visual consciousness and sensibility that would play a part in the technology-infused architecture that emerged during the latter half of the twentieth century.

The spirit of artist-architect-engineers such as Paxton and Brunel endured in structural engineers such as Peter Rice and Anthony Hunt, close collaborators in the new architecture. Rogers, who had worked with Rice on the Centre Pompidou and the Lloyd's Building, described him as 'an artist, a poet, a sculptor engineer' and acknowledged that he 'transformed the competition entry for Pompidou from a design that was in some ways too mechanistic into one that was humanistic … he was an artist and a fine mathematician. He softened the whole look of the building. There's a lot of handcraft in the building, and that's one of Peter's great contributions.'[19] The cantilevered short steel beams known as 'gerberettes' which pepper the Pompidou's distinctive facade are a case in point; Rogers recalled that 'Peter was thrilled when he came across an old Parisian lady stroking the cast steel and telling him how lovely the texture was.'[20] Shortly after winning the Pompidou competition in 1971, Rice travelled to Japan to deliver a conference paper and made a trip to

see the surviving buildings of the Osaka '70 World Expo, including the space frame structure of Kenzo Tange's Festival Plaza pavilion. 'There I saw large cast-steel nodes … an idea was born.' For Rice, the appeal of large nineteenth-century engineering structures was in the 'evidence of the attachment', for example cast-iron joints, and the care their makers had lavished on them. 'Like Gothic cathedrals, they exude craft and individual choice.'[21] Noting that cast metal had all but been abandoned as a building material since the Victorian period, Rice was determined to use cast steel as the fundamental structural material for the Centre Pompidou. It was perhaps ironic for a building to consciously express a language of standardised industrial components, while at the same time producing structural elements using a hand-crafted technique that had decades ago been eliminated by that same industrial efficiency.

Anthony Hunt had just completed his civil engineering apprenticeship in 1951 when he visited the Festival of Britain site on London's South Bank. He was particularly impressed with the soaring masted and cabled structure of Powell & Moya's Skylon, one of the centrepieces of the Festival. Inspired by this glimpse into future architectural and technical possibilities, Hunt sought employment with the structural engineers on the project, F.J. Samuely and Partners.

Working with engineer Frank Newby, who would later pioneer tensile structures such as Cedric Price's Aviary at London Zoo, Hunt enjoyed the office's close collaborative relationships between architects and engineers. He experimented with new materials such as extruded aluminium and plywood, and other industrial processes developed during the war,[22] establishing the groundwork for his later High-Tech projects that would utilise lightweight, highly engineered, component-based strategies. Hunt's vital engineering contributions run as a conduit through some of the most significant projects from this period, including the Reliance Controls Factory, the Schlumberger Research Centre, the Inmos Factory – and the Sainsbury Centre. Throughout the 1960s and 1970s, Hunt developed a number of building systems, including that for Foster Associates' IBM Pilot Head Office, a temporary building that required a flexible assembly system. According to Foster, 'the whole thing was built like a sausage, all the trades were working on site at the same time and as they completed at one end and moved down the building – so the sausage was extruded – so it was filled with people.'[23] A key collaborator on IBM was Michael Hopkins, employed at the time in the Foster office, and with whom Hunt shared a passion for sailing and yacht design. Together, they developed the SSSALU (Short Span Structures in Aluminium) building system, with yacht rigging elements used for cross-bracing and components made from extruded aluminium. The system was entirely configurable for a wide range of building types, and would later inform the structural principles of the Hopkins House and the Patera building system. The Patera project began as a commission in the late 1970s to produce ready-made workshop buildings that could emerge from a factory as prefabricated components to be bolted together on site in a matter of days. As opposed to the aluminium of the SSSALU system, here the structural cladding consisted of steel panels, and these were applied to both the walls and the roof. A similar approach can be seen in the all-encompassing cladding of the Sainsbury Centre. Attesting to its versatility, the original Patera prototype building was dismantled and re-assembled in London, where it functions today as one of the structures for the Hopkins architectural office.

Prefabricated, component-based structures such as these offered efficiencies of assembly, but also the benefits of a cleaner construction site. As Anthony Hunt attested, 'I've always hated conventional building sites … working on them is sheer misery, bloody depressing. I try to engineer buildings so that they can be pre-assembled and pieced together with the least possible fuss.' Perhaps as a reference to the core structural material of the Lloyd's Building, he admitted, 'even concrete buildings can be made to fit together neatly'. However, he added, 'although everyone would like buildings to be as precisely put together as modern cars and aircraft, in practice this is nigh impossible, unless a client is prepared to spend an absolute fortune'.[24] As exemplified by the dual industrial and hand-crafted nature of the Pompidou's gerberettes, many of these structures, although rooted in some sense of mass-produced, serial production, were necessarily part of an expensive, tailored process.

Hopkins' Patera system contains the DNA of older 'off-the-peg' construction systems that emerged in Europe and in the United States during the nineteenth and twentieth centuries. One of the earliest examples of a truly flexible, modular and prefabricated building system dates to Brunel's innovative hospital designs during the Crimean War. His rapidly assembled Renkioi Hospital (1855) was constructed just three months after the original commission, with 23 ships arriving on Turkey's Dardanelles coast, loaded with a cargo of standardised parts later compiled into a network of wooden huts.[25] Similar principles of speed and efficiency applied in the development of Ezra Ehrenkrantz's School Construction Systems Development (SCSD) project in 1962. As a response to the post-Second World War baby boom, this was intended as 'a structurally coordinated school building components system; a highly automated method of building new schools that creatively meet the needs of the ever changing educational environment through functional and flexible planning'.[26] When Norman Foster guest-edited *Architectural Review* in November 1969, he showcased the SCSD system as a model for a speculative multi-purpose building housing a factory production area, offices, storage, supermarket and a teaching space. Lessons from SCSD had already been applied to his work with Team 4 on the Reliance Controls Factory, and his proposal to 'illustrate how a single, flexible envelope can support diverse functions, like a city quarter within a single building'[27] foreshadows his Sainsbury Centre design just a few years later. Ehrenkrantz had, in turn, been influenced by British examples from the 1950s of flexible school construction, for example Alison and Peter Smithson's steel-framed Hunstanton School in Norfolk, and Erno Goldfinger's prefabricated concrete-frame schools for London County Council.

Opposite. Schlumberger
Research Centre,
Cambridge, 1982
Hopkins Architects
Anthony Hunt
Associates/
Ove Arup & Partners

Right. Snowdon Aviary,
London Zoo
Regent's Park,
London, 1964
Frank Newby, Cedric
Price & Anthony
Armstrong-Jones

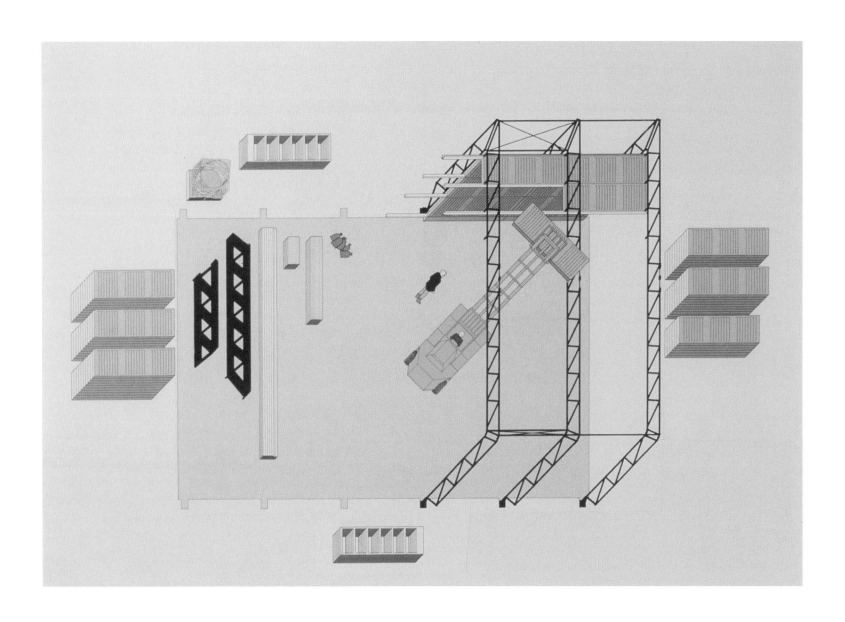

Above. Patera building
system
Drawing showing
prefabricated parts, 1982
Hopkins Architects/
Anthony Hunt Associates

Left. Hopkins
Practice Office
London, UK, 1984
Hopkins Architects/
Anthony Hunt Associates

School construction also proved influential in continental Europe. In 1949, French architect-engineer Jean Prouvé won a Ministry of Education competition to design a mass-producible rural school with classroom and teacher accommodation, resulting in two prototype buildings that were constructed in Mantoux and Bouqueval.[28] Featuring distinctive axial portal frames rendered in steel, and modular aluminium facade panels, Prouvé's demountable structure experiments began in the 1930s, as he applied extruded aluminium and sheet steel to both architecture and furniture. Just as engineers in the automobile and aeronautical industries were learning to exploit the versatility of these material processes to make safer and lighter cars and aircraft, Prouvé was exploring their potential for flexible approaches to building and construction – resulting in iconic building projects such as the Maison Tropicale (designed for colonial West Africa in 1951). Intriguingly, original examples of Prouvé's demountable buildings have enjoyed a resurgence on the auction market in recent years.[29] Undoubtedly, the relative ease of dismantling and reassembling these flexible structures has been an incentive for potential collectors.

The Maison de Verre in Paris (1932), designed by Pierre Chareau and Bernard Bijvoet, was one of the first to highlight the aesthetic potential of industrial parts – deploying elements such as hexagonal bolt-heads, rounded rivets and, most famously, a glass block facade. This created a sense of transparency while also providing a dense pattern of repeated technical components, something that engineer Peter Rice would refer to as 'scale and grain'.[30] Describing the influence of the Maison de Verre's inventory of industrial parts, Richard Rogers wrote in 1966 that 'its means of expression are pertinent to 20th century needs of mass-production and change: lightweight materials, flexible screens, steel, glass, exposed skeleton structures, rubber studded floors, Neoprene gaskets, standardised components'.[31]

Top. Perspective drawing of Bouqueval School buildings Bouqueval, France, 1949 Jean Prouvé

Above. Maison de Verre Paris, France, 1932 Pierre Chareau, Bernard Bijvoet, Louis Dalbert

'Technology transfer has all the unpredictable wonderment of genetic mutation and, in construction, its importance has been direct and seminal, although virtually unacknowledged. The auto industry, for example, has been a great source of technology transfers into building. Its cold-rolled steel chassis beams led to the birth of the family of round tubes, square tubes, angles, channels and space frame members that are widely used in construction today … the auto industry adapted the Neoprene gasket glazing developed for car windshields into a technique suitable for curtain walling systems … Complex alloy castings and large-panel raised floor systems for commercial buildings have been developed from those developed for use in large passenger aircraft.'[32]

Martin Pawley, 2000

The application of materials and methodologies from other industries such as aeronautical engineering and car design, described in the 1980s by the critic Martin Pawley as 'technology transfer', characterised projects such as the Reliance Controls Factory and the Sainsbury Centre.[33] Technology transfer facilitated a more improvisational approach to building construction, as argued for by Banham in his 1965 essay 'A Clip-On Architecture'.[34] Making the case for an architecture of indeterminate form assembled from expendable components, he referenced technology transfer in his assertion that 'the epitome of the 'clip-on' concept was the outboard motor, whose consequences for the theory of design intrigued many of us … you can convert practically any floating object into a navigable vessel.'[35]

The 'kit of parts' ethos drew from a variety of sources both within and beyond architecture. The first was in the use of stock parts; a repertoire of industrial materials used in the design of modern steel houses in mid-century California. During the 1940s, the Los Angeles-based *Arts & Architecture* magazine ran a series of competitions to find suitable designs for post-war housing. The resulting designs were all united by the recurring theme of prefabrication, and led to the influential Case Study House programme. This was a series of prototype houses built between 1945 and 1966, and designed by architects such as Craig Ellwood, Pierre Koenig, Raphael Soriano, and most famously, Charles and Ray Eames. They utilised standardised off-the-shelf components such as corrugated steel sheets, and employed agile wartime production processes such as arc welding, all in an attempt to reduce costs and to seek efficiencies of assembly. In an interview with the Los Angeles Herald-Examiner in 1960, describing the components used in his Stahl House (Case Study House No. 22), Koenig explained, 'I never have steel fabricated especially to my design – I use only stock parts. That is the challenge – to take these common everyday parts and work them into an aesthetically pleasing concept.' Looking at the utilitarian corrugated steel cladding and elegant cross-bracing of Team 4's Reliance Controls Factory, one can immediately see the direct lineage from these iconic Californian designs. Richard Rogers once stated, 'You know how key [Raphael] Soriano was to me – from Reliance, to Beaubourg [Pompidou], and Lloyd's'.[36]

A project that explicitly expressed these ideas, and on a compact scale, was Richard Horden's Yacht House (1984), which used fittings from boat shops and yacht suppliers. Taking the tubular aluminium yacht mast as its fundamental building element, Horden structured this family home around a single-storey 'wind frame', with

Stahl House
Case Study House No. 22
Los Angeles, USA, 1959
Pierre Koenig

Opposite. Eames House
Case Study House No. 8
Los Angeles, USA, 1949
Charles and Ray Eames

a modular plan that could easily expand as needs evolved.[37] Yacht masts became architectural columns, oval-section spars became beams, rigging became cross-bracing, sails became canopies, and deck hatches became rooflights. It took just over five hours to erect the 20-bay frame, and with a construction crew more familiar with boats than with buildings.[38]

In addition to the use of stock parts and materials, architects also looked to other means of industrial production to inform their ideas of prefabrication. As previously noted, Buckminster Fuller's Dymaxion House was an early example of house design to adopt principles of production from the automobile industry. Conceived during the 1920s as a response to housing shortages in Europe and America following the First World War, the octagonal Dymaxion housing units were designed to be factory-produced and cost-efficient. Originally exhibited at the Marshall Fields department store in Chicago in 1929, each boasted prefabricated wall units that acted as movable space dividers, and prefabricated bathroom modules – an idea later exploited in Grimshaw's Service Tower (1967) and in the Lloyd's Building's external bathroom modules. Both projects demonstrate a 'kit of parts' aesthetic common with the Dymaxion concept, and a distinctive quality that Pawley described as 'maximum inventory: minimum diversity architecture', i.e. the minimum application of the maximum number of components.[39]

The Hauer-King House, designed in 1994 by Future Systems, has traces of both the Dymaxion concept and the Maison de Verre, with its freestanding storage pods and brightly coloured bathroom enclosed within a facade of glazed bricks. It was described at the time as 'made from pieces that seem fused together into solid art. Like a Bugatti, a J-Class yacht, a Henry Moore or a Spitfire, the house is an assembly that, once comprehended, can never again be wholly dismantled in the mind into constituent parts.'[40] The co-founder of

Top. Yacht House
New Forest, UK, 1983
Richard Horden/
Horden Cherry Lee
Architects

Above. Dymaxion House
Kansas City, USA, 1941
Richard Buckminster
Fuller, built by Butler
Brothers, Kansas City
Originally conceived
in the 1920s, various
versions were built in
the 1940s.

Left. Hauer-King House
London, UK, 1994
Future Systems

Future Systems, Jan Kaplický, was part of the Rogers/Piano team that designed the Centre Pompidou, and he later worked in Norman Foster's office. He was known during the 1970s and 1980s for his visionary architectural drawings of experimental structures such as the Doughnut House (1986), a project described as 'a domestic house drawn as a weird subterranean machine'[41] and which clearly paid homage to Buckminster Fuller's Dymaxion units. One of Kaplický's few built projects, the Stirling Prize-winning Media Centre for Lord's Cricket Ground (completed with partner Amanda Levete) contained the essence of his drawings of lightweight structures while also demonstrating technology transfer. It was the world's first all-aluminium, semi-monocoque structure (the combination of tensile stressed skin with internal ribbed frame). Built by boatyard specialists, it borrowed techniques from hull design and racing car construction. Kaplický believed that adopting these technologies could 'give energy to the spirit of architecture by introducing a new generation of buildings which are efficient, elegant, versatile and exciting … based on the celebration of technology, not the concealment of it.'[42]

The crisp, graphic quality of Kaplický's axonometric drawings seem reminiscent of the iconic cut-away drawings that filled the pages of the Eagle comic which Norman Foster has cited as an influence on his decision to take up architecture. Referring to the detailed renderings of machinery, aircraft and spaceships that accompanied the adventures of Dan Dare, 'Pilot of the Future', Foster stated, 'I loved the coloured, cross-sectional, technical drawings'.[43] The comic's imagery of futuristic cities and fantastical technology certainly infuses the sleek spaceship contours of the Sainsbury Centre, and Foster even commissioned Eagle artist John Batchelor to draw his Renault Distribution Centre as a pull-out poster for *Architectural Review* in July 1983.

Advances in space technology also informed a concept of architecture as a complete system into which the necessary means of environmental control and life support could be 'plugged in.' Archigram's utopian proposals for modular construction, flexible internal programmes, and a demountability achieved through 'clip-on' and 'plug-in' structures reflected contemporary advances in technology associated with jet-age aeronautical design, and outer space habitability studies, for example Raymond Loewy's work on NASA's Skylab space station project. Archigram's 'Capsule Homes' and 'Plug-in City' projects (both 1964), seemed to have been snatched straight from the pages of Dan Dare. The pages of their eponymous magazine were laden with machine-conscious imagery. *Archigram* no. 4 (1964), the famous 'Zoom' issue, explored 'the relationship between architecture, science fiction, science fact, and comics'[44] and featured a centrefold with a pop-up sci-fi cityscape that sought the 'breakdown of conventional attitudes, the disruption of the

Lord's Cricket Ground
Media Centre
London, UK, 1999
Future Systems

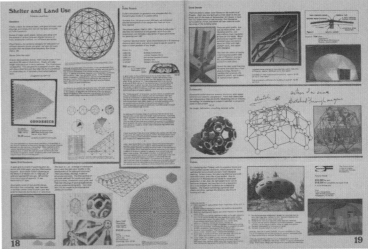

Left. Renault
Distribution Centre
Interior perspective
cutaway drawing by
John Batchelor
Published in
Architectural Review,
July 1983
Swindon, UK, 1982
Foster Associates/
Ove Arup & Partners

Above. *Whole Earth
Catalog*, 'Shelter and
Land Use', Fall 1969

'straight-up-and-down' formal vacuum – necessary to create a
more dynamic environment'.[45]

Just as new material technologies enabled architectural
experimentation during the 1960s and 1970s, so too did new low-cost
printing technologies (such as portable mimeograph machines) allow for
the proliferation of radical magazines such as *Archigram*, thus acting as
a catalyst for the breakthrough construction materials and processes
just around the corner. Other magazines in a similar vein highlighted
the DIY potential of the 'kit of parts' ethos, as well as projecting how
new communications technologies might also enhance the designed
environment. In the US, the influential *Whole Earth Catalog* (1968–72),
founded by counter-cultural guru Stewart Brand, advocated for a
wholesale 'access to tools' by publishing information on how to build
your own dome homes or low-tech earth shelters.[46] Back in the UK,
the DIY turn was captured in Charles Jencks and Nathan Silver's book
Adhocism: The Case for Improvisation, published in 1972, and featuring
Silver's Adhocist chair on the cover, made from industrial parts including
a tractor seat, bicycle and wheelchair components, and gas pipes.

Right. Cover of
*Adhocism: The Case
for Improvisation*, by
Charles Jencks and
Nathan Silver, first
published 1972. The
Ad Hoc Chair, featured
on the cover, was
designed by Silver
and manufactured by
Crofton Engineering Ltd.

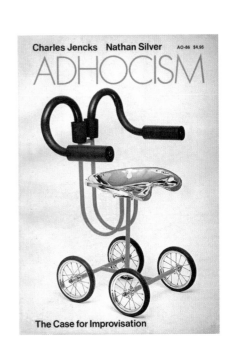

Utopias and megastructures

Describing the utopian imagery produced by Archigram and their peers, architect Denise Scott Brown observed in 1968, 'Many of these cities do look familiar … like the industrial outskirts of American cities, like Jersey tank farms and cracking towers, or the oil derricks, pumps and cranes of San Pedro harbour.'[47]

Scott Brown's observation points once again to the long tradition of engineering embedded in the 1960s visual projection of the future. Yet the images also evoked a kind of technological expressionism which forms part of the long history of Modernism. An early precedent for this architectural fascination with the visual tropes of technology is evident in the fantastical urban projects by Italian Futurists, Antonio Sant'Elia and Mario Chiattone (1914), and Russian Constructivist, Iakov Chernikov (1933). As with Archigram, these schemes looked both backwards and forwards. They remained tantalisingly unbuilt but became renowned through publication. These drawings portray buildings that feel like pure engineering structure, with uninterrupted steel girder forms that reach vertiginous heights, and sleek paper-thin facades that predict the technological capabilities of materials that would be developed many decades later.[48]

In *Theory and Design in the First Machine Age* (1960) Banham had called upon architects to recover this alternative Modernist tradition, by 'emulating the Futurists' in stretching the definition of architecture. The vision of the city as a kind of technological megastructure – plugged-in, mobile, adaptive and impermanent – helped to inform the development of proto-High Tech projects. Banham looked to exemplars of radical practice such as the 1920s Soviet Constructivist idea of architecture as a 'social condenser' – in which hierarchies of social behaviour would be broken down through communal arrangement of services.

1960s radical architects were in tune with this idea of making new forms of social interaction through the design of adaptive environments. Cedric Price's 'Fun Palace' (1964), designed as a 'short-term plaything' in collaboration with theatre director Joan Littlewood, was perhaps the most influential unbuilt project of the decade, and a direct influence upon the design of Centre Pompidou.[49] This proposal for an interactive mixed-use education and cultural space was a compelling blend of Price's ludic attitude to the city and Littlewood's track record in improvised participatory theatre. The Fun Palace's colossal structural frame and plugged-in units bore a resemblance to Basil Spence's Sea and Ships Pavilion at the 1951 Festival of Britain, which had featured exposed trusses, lightweight clipped-on panels, and loosely angled partitions – resulting in a visually dynamic and open facade arrangement. The Fun Palace, equipped with information screens and a flexible framework with 'plug-in' programmable spaces, clearly provided a road map for the Centre Pompidou's ambitions for adaptability over a decade later. Utopian proposals such as Archigram's Plug-in City and Price's Fun Palace found an almost immediate built realisation at the 1970 Osaka Expo, with Kenzo Tange's Festival Plaza pavilion and its extendible space frame outfitted with demountable capsule units and entertainment robots. Dennis Crompton, one of Archigram's founders, recalled that he enjoyed his visit to the Expo because 'it was the first time many of those ideas appeared in built form.'[50]

Right. Archigram, 'A Walking City' (proposal for New York City), 1964
Drawing by Ron Herron

Opposite.
Antonio Sant'Elia 'The New City', 1914, detail
Ink over black pencil on paper

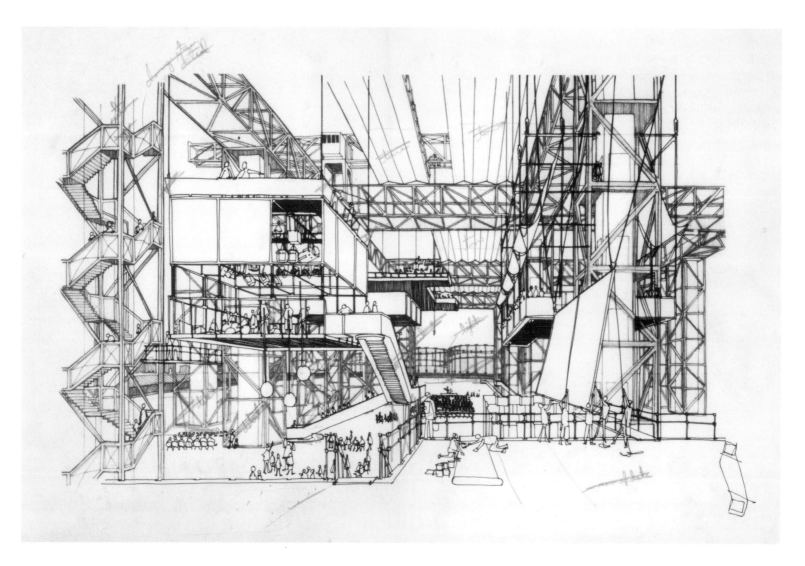

Osaka '70 was the culmination of a decade of utopian research from a group of Japanese architects, led by Tange, who had launched their 'Metabolist' manifesto at the 1960 World Design Conference in Tokyo. Like Archigram, the Metabolists were looking for new ways to build cities and communities during this period of post-war economic recovery and growth, and many of their ideas evolved along parallel lines. The Metabolist name referenced the architectural possibilities for organic growth and response to the environment, to hint at the idea of impermanence and constant change – a design strategy that avoided fixed forms and functions. For example, Arata Isozaki's 'Clusters in The Air' project (1960–2) proposed arranging housing units in groups that appeared like leaves on a tree, with passageways acting as branches to link together clusters of living pods, and these trees interconnecting to form an urban 'forest'. Many Metabolist projects embraced the concept of the 'megastructure' – a densely massed conglomeration of architectural forms with the inherent potential for extendability and adaptability. One of the Metabolists, Fumihiko Maki, was the first to coin the term, in 1964. He defined the megastructure as 'a large frame in which all functions of a city are housed … made possible by present day technology … it is a man-made feature of the landscape, like the great hills on which Italian towns are built.' Describing the 'utility in combination and concentration of function' of the megastructure frame concept, he hastened to sound a note of warning that 'technology must not dictate choices to us in our cities' and that we should not 'confuse the potential of technology with a compulsion to use it fully'.[51]

In his seminal 1976 book on megastructures, and referring to a visual language later witnessed in the densely complex, animated facades of 'megastructural' projects such as the Centre Pompidou, Lloyd's Building and Hong Kong and Shanghai Bank Headquarters, Reyner Banham noted that 'the younger megastructuralists saw technology as a visually wild rich mess of piping and wiring and struts and catwalks and bristling radar antennae and supplementary fuel tanks and landing-pads all carried in exposed lattice frames, NASA-style.'[52] This playful appropriation of machine imagery can be seen in the work of the avant-garde Austrian architectural group, Zünd-Up, whose 'Great Vienna Auto-Expander' parking garage proposal (1969) featured soaring steel frame supports and gigantic fragments of muscle car engines 'clipped on', with glistening chrome pistons and cylinders towering over the city. Running side by side with Chernikov's *Architectural Fantasies* (1933) and the Lloyd's Building (1986) one might also consider cinema's fascination with the 'wild, rich mess' of technology and industry, for example the subterranean factory scenes from *Metropolis* (1927), or the labyrinthine ducting and elevated walkways of the Japanese 'megacity' depicted in the anime film, *Ghost In The Shell* (1995). In fact, an image of the factory machinery from *Metropolis* had been included in a spread in the sci-fi-themed 'Zoom' issue of the *Archigram* magazine.

Ten years after Osaka '70, members of Archigram (accompanied by Cedric Price) embarked on a bus trip to visit the completed Centre

Opposite, top left.
Sea and Ships Pavilion,
Festival of Britain
South Bank, London, 1951
Basil Spence & Partners/
Freeman Fox & Partners
View from the rear of the
Dome of Discovery.

Opposite, top right.
Arata Isozaki
Sketch for 'Clusters in
the Air' (unbuilt project
for Tokyo), c.1960–2
Pen and black ink

Opposite, bottom.
Cedric Price
Fun Palace, interior
perspective, c.1964
Pink and green pencil
on reprographic copy

Right. Festival Plaza
Expo '70, Osaka, 1970
Kenzo Tange, Arata
Isozaki, Atsushi Ueda
Tange was Chief
Architect of the Expo,
while Isozaki and Ueda
were responsible for the
Festival Plaza.

Pompidou. Around this time, Banham had described the Pompidou as a 'full-scale Archigram drawing',[53] and indeed the building's dynamic facade embodied much of the functional colour coding that was characteristic of Archigram's iconic rendering. It perhaps most explicitly referenced their 1968 'Oasis' project for a multi-functional civic and cultural 'laboratory' – 'with its slogans of emancipation and choice, the 'fun' structure invades, liberates, displaces the architecture of the conventional city'.[54] The tour group from Archigram acknowledged that the Pompidou was 'a formalised example of their architecture' – the closest thing they had seen to a constructed version of their theoretical propositions.[55] However, they also expressed disappointment in how the flexibility – suggested in the original concept design – was in reality rather constrained. They concluded that the Pompidou, despite the visual metaphors for circulation and exchange, remained fundamentally a static building.[56] Reflecting upon the project's original lofty aspirations and the influence of the Fun Palace's cross-functional public purpose, Richard Rogers would wistfully describe the initial Pompidou proposal as 'the British Museum crossed with Times Square'.[57] The Fun Palace was rare amongst megastructural projects due to the absence of fixed floor levels. Endorsing full interchangeability and extension, the structure's massive open frame gave it the dimensions of a shipyard,

along with the shipping and cargo industry's tools and visual cues – for example, the Fun Palace was to have fifteen latticed steel towers, each connected at their head by trackways to carry travelling gantry cranes capable of transporting equipment to all parts of the site, allowing it to be infinitely configurable. No doubt this structural and functional flexibility allowed the proposal to be sited in any number of potential locations – something that would have helped during the project's initial advocacy phase, to find willing partners and funders. According to Price, 'the sense of confinement on the site is reduced by the deliberate extension of the visible limits … the activities should be experimental, the place itself expendable and changeable … the organisation of the space and objects occupying it should allow for a flow of space and time, in which passive and active pleasure is provoked.'[58] Many of these attributes would be seen a decade later in the concept designs by Piano + Rogers for Pompidou. Commenting on the building in the *Architectural Review*, Banham acknowledged the presence of the Fun Palace's ghost, and declared that the Centre Pompidou had 'the honour of being the most complete realisation of the megastructure dream.'[59]

In Japan, Metabolist Kisho Kurokawa's Nakagin Capsule Tower (1968–72) was another realisation of the megastructure dream. It blended elements of Archigram's Plug-in City and Cedric Price's Thinkbelt crate housing proposal, the latter part of a radical project to regenerate England's post-industrial Potteries region by employing neglected infrastructure to create a new hub of higher education focused on engineering and technology. Kurokawa's mixed-use residential and office project represented a late flowering of the Metabolist movement, and remains one of its few surviving built examples, although sadly it has recently been threatened with demolition. The tower consists of a concrete and steel superstructure 'plugged in' with an array of prefabricated units, each consisting of a steel-trussed box complete with built-in bed and dropped-in bathroom module. The units were assembled off site and hoisted into place by cranes – evoking the visionary schemes by Archigram and Price. The Thinkbelt proposal had featured the use of rail-mounted gantry cranes to service short-term portable enclosures (echoing the Fun Palace), and the re-deployment of train carriages as mobile lecture rooms.[60] As with similar Japanese 'capsule hotels', Kurokawa's Capsule Tower was conceived as cheap temporary accommodation for businessmen forgoing their commute home. The

project borrowed elements from Kiyonori Kikutake's 'plugged-in' Festival Tower at the Osaka '70 Expo, while also adopting principles from the shipping industry, reconfiguring industrial materials such as cargo containers to create a flexible solution that could adapt to the dense urban context of Tokyo's Ginza district.[61] During the late 1980s and early 1990s, Richard Rogers developed two cultural and residential projects for similarly tight urban sites in Tokyo (Kabuki-Cho Tower and Tomigaya) both of which were products of Japan's property boom at the time, and demonstrated the advantages of applying these industry-led building strategies to highly challenging, compact city contexts.

According to Banham, the ideal 'megastructure' should be 'composed of several independent systems that can expand or contract with the least disturbance to the others [rather than] one rigid hierarchical system … each system which makes the whole maintains its identity, while at the same time engaged in dynamic contact with the others … permitting the greatest efficiency and flexibility with the smallest organisational structure.'[62] An early prototype for these ideas – clustering functions and programme, and massing them into some

Cedric Price
Drawing of crate housing for Potteries Thinkbelt project (unbuilt), c.1963–7
Black ink on tracing paper

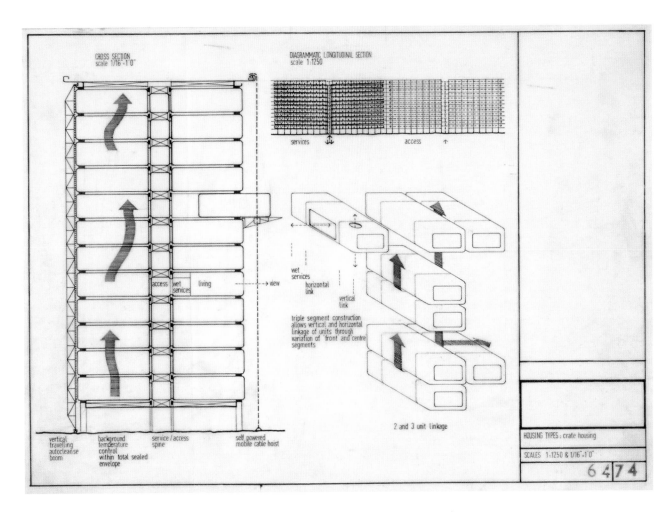

Joseph Paxton
Design for the 'Great
Victorian Way' (unbuilt),
1855
Pencil, pen, ink and
watercolour

kind of technologically advanced man-made landform – can be seen in Joseph Paxton's visionary proposal for the 'Great Victorian Way' in 1855. Perhaps the world's first example of a 'megastructure' using modern materials, this unrealised project was for an iron and glass orbital infrastructure loop around London. Paxton took the template from the transept of his 1851 Crystal Palace and extruded this along a 10-mile path that roughly followed the route of today's Circle Line. Sealed off from London's climate and pollution, the sheltered transport spine integrated pedestrian walkways, 'omnibuses and passenger carriages',[63] and an elevated pneumatic railway, with luxury residences and an array of high-end shops. This image of a sprawling, glazed structure winding its way through the city would be revived a century later with Misha Black's equally ambitious concept proposal for a vast complex on the South Bank for the Festival of Britain. Londoners would have witnessed this megastructure stretching along the riverbank from the County Hall building all the way to Bankside Power Station, featuring a 'great spiral ramp' and flexible framework from which 'the buildings rise in terraces to the sky platform fifteen

hundred feet above London'.[64] Just as Paxton was seeking a solution to alleviate the city's increasing transport congestion with his efficient orbital loop, Black's proposal (although never built) considered issues of mass-mobility – incorporating a network of elevated walkways and spiralling vehicle ramps populated with cars twisting their way around and through the riverside megastructure. Similar intentions lie at the heart of Paul Rudolph's controversial Lower Manhattan Expressway project (1970). This gargantuan concrete superhighway integrated housing, sunken roadways and elevated mass-transit monorails, but would have cut a fatal swathe through historic neighbourhoods including SoHo and Little Italy. Rudolph, of course, taught Foster and the Rogers at Yale in the early 60s. Traces of Rudolph's unbuilt project can also be discerned in the megastructural strategies of Denys Lasdun's ziggurat buildings for the University of East Anglia. Snaking their way alongside the site of the Sainsbury Centre, these student accommodation units were described at the time of conception as a 'daring new experiment' and were proposed around the same time that Cedric Price was formulating his Potteries

Thinkbelt proposal, a similar attempt to reconceptualise British universities. At the press conference in 1963 unveiling Lasdun's proposed designs, Frank Thistlethwaite (UEA's first vice-chancellor) outlined the implementation of 'flexibility and coherence' that would facilitate future expansion – of both student numbers and physical structures – for this ambitious, new university. Speaking to a journalist during the event, Lasdun stated, 'We have envisaged it as a tightly organised complex of buildings in which people can move freely over this beautiful site, rubbing shoulders with each other, and exchanging ideas, and we've done everything in our plan to assist it.'[65]

These multiple sources did not pave the way solely for High Tech. Despite common roots, the confluence of ideas around adaptive technologies, both 'low' and 'high' tech, as well as the megastructural possibilities of the future city, split in different directions. In some quarters, the techno-utopian thinking of the 1960s took a more nihilistic turn, for example in Italy, where radical groups such as Superstudio and Archizoom became increasingly critical of architecture's capacity to effect social change through technological advancement. By the 1970s, this techno-utopianism was felt by some to be out of kilter with a shift in environmental debates, and an economic downturn brought about by, amongst other things, the ensuing oil crisis in the early years of that decade. Charles Jencks' famous proclamation of the death of Modernism – which he located to the moment of demolition of Minoru Yamasaki's Pruitt-Igoe housing project in St Louis, Missouri on March 15, 1972 – has generally been held to mark the end of the megastructural idea and a utopian faith in Modernist planning. And yet, technological Modernism proved to be as adaptive as its structures were intended to be, as the success of High Tech in the ensuing decades was to show.

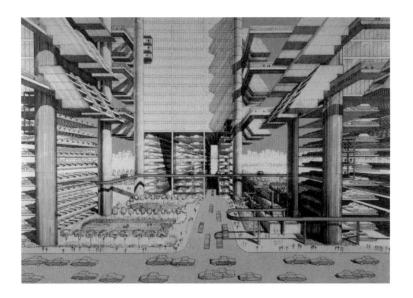

Above. Paul Rudolph
Lower Manhattan
Expressway project
(unbuilt), c.1967–72
Perspective rendering
of streetscape

Below. Norfolk and
Suffolk Terrace
(Ziggurats), University
of East Anglia student
campus
Norwich, UK, 1964–8
Denys Lasdun & Partners

The corporate ideal

As plans for the Sainsbury Centre were being made for Norwich, Foster Associates were putting the completing touches to an office building in nearby Ipswich, for the Willis Faber & Dumas insurance company (1972–5), who were relocating their staff to a cheaper, provincial site outside of London. Squeezed onto a tight site in the historic market town, the building is a four-storey office block arranged around a colourful central atrium with a bank of escalators given deep open-plan access to all floors. A ground-floor swimming pool and rooftop garden and restaurant provided attractive amenities designed to entice the relocated workers. The technical efficiency of the building was provided by the innovative use of a raised 'aircraft' floor containing cables and services. The building was wrapped in a sheath of brown tinted glass (the same toughened glass used in car windshields), giving a mirror effect during daytime (reflecting the older buildings surrounding it) and 'disappearing' at night when lit from inside. Like Reliance Controls, Foster was aiming for a democratisation of the workspace through open circulation and social facilities.

Willis Faber & Dumas was one of a number of projects in the 1970s which showed how technological modernism could meet the needs of new corporate approaches. Not surprisingly, perhaps, High Tech architects were engaged by corporations faced with rethinking their corporate structures and operations through a systems design approach. For example, Foster's design for the IBM Pilot Office in Cosham (1971) was a tough brief for an inexpensive single storey office to cater for up to 1000 employees, whilst a new permanent headquarters was built nearby. Housing the services and extensive computer cabling within a raised floor, roof and inside the structural supports allowed for all the building's requirements to be contained in a flexible, single structure, just as Reliance Controls had done.

The advanced office and factory complexes of the 1970s pointed to another key direction shaping British architecture in the 1980s – the growth of the research facility. This is where the meaning of High Tech comes into its own – not as a singular stylistic idiom, but a marriage of architecture with the advanced practices of high tech industries. Rogers + Piano designed the British headquarters of American company PA Technology in Cambridgeshire in 1975, using a 'kit of parts' approach, and a steel frame with interchangeable glass and insulated sandwich cladding. The project let to another, the Rogers-designed PA Laboratories or 'Patscentre' in Princeton, New Jersey (1982–5). The Patscentre featured a coloured masted structure that Rogers also employed for the Inmos microprocessor factory in

Top. Willis Faber &
Dumas Limited
Ipswich, UK, 1975
Foster Associates/
Anthony Hunt Associates

Above. IBM Pilot
Headquarters
Cosham, UK, 1971
Foster Associates/
Anthony Hunt Associates

Left. PATMOS,
Patscentre
Princeton, USA, 1985
Richard Rogers
Partnership,
Kelbaugh and Lee
Architects/
Ove Arup & Partners

Below. Inmos
Microprocessor Factory
Newport, UK, 1987
Richard Rogers
Partnership/
Anthony Hunt Associates

Newport, South Wales (1982), designed with engineer Peter Rice.
A different masted strategy was employed by Hopkins for the design
of the Schlumberger research facility in Cambridge (1985), this time
supporting a billowing, Teflon-coated fabric roof covering a drilling rig
test station and an airy 'winter-garden' which provided the company's
social space. Lightweight, economic masted structures were also
employed in the design of projects such as Rogers' Fleetguard factory
in Quimper, France (1979) and Foster's Renault Distribution Centre in
Swindon (1982).

High-tech research facilities, production and distribution sites
were often the result of British government encouragement of new
industries in areas targeted for industrial redevelopment or growth,
such as the M4 corridor between London and South Wales, or the
emerging 'Silicon Fen' area of Cambridgeshire. Across Britain, and
particularly in the South East, business parks and out-of-town retail
and leisure facilities sprouted with masted and canopied sheds and
glazed boxes, as these design tropes were adopted by commercial
developers. Whilst such developments ignored the organisational
logic and research-driven objectives of the architects they sought to
emulate, the 1980s and 1990s saw a kind of domestication of High
Tech style which is still evident in the British landscape today.

Left. Lloyd's of London
London, UK, 1986
Richard Rogers
Partnership/
Ove Arup & Partners

Opposite. Hong Kong
& Shanghai Bank
Headquarters
Hong Kong, China,
1986
Foster Associates/
Ove Arup & Partners

As the recession of the 1970s faded, technological Modernism also found favour with corporations redesigning their image in light of a new order of global finance. During the 1980s, business practices were reshaped by both the property 'boom' and the 'big bang' in financial operations and information technology. Institutions such as the insurance trading body Lloyd's of London, for example, had to accommodate their historic associations (dating back to the late seventeenth century) with the fast pace of technological change affecting global business. Not only that, but it had to do so on a difficult site in the heart of London's financial district. Richard Rogers' solution incorporated existing elements, such as the grand arched portal on Leadenhall Street, and the Robert Adam-designed dining/committee room (originally from Bowood House) into a spectacular and complex concrete structure (as required by fire authorities) of multiple service towers clad in steel, with external glazed lift access, allowing for a central atrium with uninterrupted floor space for offices and trading. The atrium was topped with a glazed, latticed arch which referenced Paxton's Crystal Palace. Like Pompidou, the building was a visible expression of movement and change – only this time the dynamic impression was one of big business at work.

In a parallel development, Norman Foster's design for an office tower for the Hong Kong and Shanghai Bank (now HSBC) in the former British colony, was for a landmark, high-rise construction that would address the changing nature of financial operations, and act as a symbol of prestige. The design features a suspension structure supporting three interlinked towers, the tallest of which is 44 storeys. The high degree of prefabrication employed was also a response to the demand for speed of construction. The HSBC building had, famously, to incorporate the principles of *feng shui* in its design, thus demonstrating how tradition and modernity collided in the corporate visions of the late twentieth century.

Following on from the iconic 1980s examples such as the Lloyd's building and the Hong Kong and Shanghai Bank headquarters, the use of certain High Tech tropes – for example the muscular expression of engineering joints and the sleek appearance of razor-thin facades – maintained a certain cachet amongst corporate office buildings well into the twenty-first century. Just as the image of the glazed curtain wall personified the corporate Modernism of the post-war period, in buildings like SOM's Lever House (designed by Gordon Bunshaft and completed in 1952), the High Tech high-rise office complex has shaped the skyline of our cities at the turn of the twenty-first century.

Conclusion

The adaptability of technological Modernism or High Tech, as it became known, to corporate interest has been much remarked upon, and criticised, in an age of post-crash economics. Similarly, the early technological obsessiveness, forged in the utopian crucible of late 1960s experimentalism, has come under attack for its adherence to a techno-futurist vision which has been challenged by environmental and sustainability concerns. Architects have answered this by demonstrating how environmental factors may be met through continued experimentation with lightweight structures and a 'serviced' approach to building – witness Grimshaw's iconic biodomes of the Eden Project (2001), or Hopkins' design for the Dynamic Earth Centre in Edinburgh, Scotland (1999).

For a brief period too, it seemed as if some of the principles behind High-Tech architecture – i.e. flexible, rapid assembly construction systems, modular grid plans, adaptability and extendability – might also be applied to certain extreme environments that would imminently be explored and conquered by mankind. In 1984, Jan Kaplický wrote an article for *The Architectural Review*[66] outlining the possibilities for architects in the wake of President

Reagan's commitment to building a permanently manned space station within the decade. After all, the gradual 'construction-by-accretion' nature of long-term space structures might seem perfectly suited for the 'plug-in' and 'clip-on' methodologies of High Tech. Kaplický described how the space station's central habitation module would need to adapt to multiple functions, including sleeping, eating and relaxation, as the surrounding modules would be turned over to scientific and operational duties. He also noted that every item used to equip the interiors of these modules would need to be small enough to pass through the narrow airlocks at either end of the modules – an observation that brings to mind the thin rod-like connectors between the pod segments of Archigram's Plug-in City concept. A few years later, Kaplický would state that in the twenty-first century, 'systems derived from advanced space applications will initiate a new generation of structural concepts back on Earth.' Referring to NASA's space station research, he described how 'prototype beam-builder machines developed for automatic fabrication of space structures can be used to construct lightweight envelopes in remote terrestrial regions where normal construction techniques

Below. Eden Project
Bodelva, UK, 2001
Nicholas Grimshaw &
Partners/
Anthony Hunt Associates

Right. Dynamic
Earth Centre
Edinburgh, UK, 1999
Hopkins Architects/
Ove Arup & Partners

Above. International
Terminal Waterloo
London, UK, 1993
Nicholas Grimshaw &
Partners/
Anthony Hunt Associates/
Cass Hayward &
Partners/Tony Gee
& Partners/
Red de Ferrocarriles
Británicos

Top. Halley VI British
Antarctic Research
Station for British
Antarctic Survey
Brunt Ice Shelf,
Antarctica, 2005–13
Hugh Broughton
Architects/
AECOM

are impossible.'[67] This notion of a nimble, deployable construction
system echoes the labour-saving devices used for the Crystal Palace
(such as the 'sash bar machines' used to cut standardised lengths of
timber) and also highlights fabrication technologies of today, such as
3D printing and rapid prototyping, which we now see being applied
to full-scale architectural construction. In 2013, Foster + Partners
unveiled designs, created in collaboration with the European Space
Agency, to construct a habitation base on the Moon that would be
3D printed using lunar soil. Perhaps the closest thing we have seen to
Kaplický's 'new generation of structural concepts' is Hugh Broughton
Architects' designs for the Halley VI British Antarctic Survey research
station (2005–13). These eye-catching primary-coloured red and blue
interconnected pods use hydraulic legs and skis to allow them to be
relocated away from snowdrifts and the shifting ice shelf. They give
the impression of dwellings straight out of a sci-fi comic, and display
more than a passing resemblance to Archigram's 'Walking City'
project. There have been a number of other architectural competitions
for Antarctic research stations in recent years, and so this may be
an area of future development for proto-High-Tech projects. As the
architect and critic Sam Jacob has observed, 'the history of Antarctic
architecture seems a hyper-accelerated history of architecture itself,
progressing from the hut to the space station in just over a hundred
years'.[68] Intriguingly, Hopkins Architects also submitted a design for
the Halley VI competition, with a concept based on Brunel's 1855 prefabricated modular hospital in the Crimea.

In the mid-1990s, Charles Jencks noted a 'softening' of
High Tech in what he described as a move towards 'Organi-tech'.
Observing the emergence of new sinuous forms and complex organic
shapes (perhaps a return to the tendril-like structural forms of the Iron

Bridge over two centuries previously?), Jencks acknowledged the new design possibilities that had been facilitated by computer-aided design at the start of the decade, enabling a shift away from the more rectilinear and rigid geometries that High Tech was known for during the 1970s and 1980s. 'A slide in emphasis … but technology and utilitarian concerns still predominate … in primary place is still repetition, the shed, utility, and yes, the Machine Aesthetic, even if it is less aggressive than at the Pompidou Center.' He recognised the 'commitment to the curve' from Spanish architect-engineer, Santiago Calatrava, with the soaring struts and trusses of his railway station halls and river bridges. With perhaps a slightly pessimistic tone, he stated that 'a biomorphic turn is possible, but it is unlikely, given the obligation of High-Tech architects to express the regularity and rationality of structure.' However, he did mark out Nicholas Grimshaw's recently completed Waterloo International Terminal (1993) as an example of how architecture could find a way forward, taking the 'kit of parts' from High Tech while seeking newer forms of ambiguity and nuance. Jencks stated that the Waterloo project 'uses structure as a changing, oppositional set of systems … they fly about in a ballet of give and take, the very image of living form.'[69]

We can still see today countless examples of High Tech's industrial-conscious legacy, whether in the almost ubiquitous use of shipping containers in retail parks and residential projects,[70] or in the quick-build private homes designed using off-the-shelf industrial materials and assembly systems that we see on TV architecture makeover shows.[71]

It seems that Kaplický's initial observations about the fundamental lessons to be learned from High Tech still hold true, namely that this was never just a question of style, but rather a consequence of taking advantage of technological progress: 'Here are some new technological ingredients which can be used to construct the future … ultimately, the design limits will be set, not by the capability of the technology involved, but by the depth of our creative imaginations.'[72]

Multi-dome lunar base
under construction
(concept rendering)
Lunar 3D Printing
Project, 2013
European Space Agency/
Foster + Partners

Notes

1 Reyner Banham, *Theory and Design in the First Machine Age* (London: The Architectural Press, 1960), pp. 329–30.

2 See Todd Gannon, *Reyner Banham and the Paradoxes of High Tech* (Los Angeles: The Getty Research Centre, 2017).

3 Philip Johnson, quoted in Murray Fraser with Joe Kerr, *Architecture and the 'Special Relationship': The American Influence on Post-War British Architecture* (Oxford and New York: Routledge, 2007), p. 315.

4 Witold Rybczynski, *The Biography of a Building: How Robert Sainsbury and Norman Foster Built a Great Museum* (London: Thames & Hudson, 2011) p. 106.

5 Rybczynski, *Biography of a Building*, p. 140.

6 Buckminster Fuller, Royal Gold Medal Conclusion, quoted in *On Foster ... Foster On*, ed. by David Jenkins (Munich, London and New York: Prestel, 2000), p. 131.

7 Charles Jencks, quoted in Jenkins, *On Foster ... Foster On*, p. 57.

8 Reyner Banham, 'High Tech and Advanced Engineering' *c.*1987, in *Reyner Banham Papers*, acc. no. 910009, box 8, folder 3, Getty Research Institute, Los Angeles. This unpublished manuscript is included in Gannon, *Reyner Banham and the Paradoxes of High Tech*, pp. 223–46. Quotation appears on p. 244.

9 Peter Buchanan, 'High-Tech: Another British Thoroughbred', *The Architectural Review*, Issue 174, 1983, pp. 15–19.

10 Charles Jencks, 'Postmodern vs Late-Modern' in *Zeitgeist in Babel: The Postmodernist Controversy*, ed. by Ingeborg Hoesterey (Bloomington and Indianapolis: Indiana University Press, 1991) p. 16.

11 Richard Rogers, quoted in Kenneth Powell, *Richard Rogers: Complete Works Volume 1* (London: Phaidon, 1999) p. 56.

12 Reyner Banham, 'A Clip-On Architecture', Design Quarterly No. 63, 1965; reprinted in *Architectural Design* Vol. 25, 1965, pp. 534–5.

13 Nicholas Grimshaw, film featuring the Service Tower at <https://grimshaw.global/projects/service-tower-for-student-housing/> [accessed 14 February 2018].

14 Simon Sadler in Mark Crinson and Claire Zimmerman, *Neo-avant-garde and Postmodern: Postwar Architecture in Britain and Beyond* (Studies in British Art 21), (New Haven and London: Yale, 2010) p. 371.

15 'The Britain that is going to be forged in the white heat of this revolution will be no place for restrictive practices or for outdated methods on either side of industry'. Harold Wilson, speech at the Labour Party Conference (1 October 1963), quoted in *Labour Party Annual Conference Report 1963*, pp. 139–40.

16 Jonathan Glancey, 'Engineering a Thing of Beauty', interview with engineer Anthony Hunt in *The Independent*, 23 January 1991, p. 17.

17 The Ironbridge Museum Trust was established in 1967, for example. The historian of technology, L.T.C. Rolt, was a founder member and the author of popular books on Brunel (1957) and Telford (1967).

18 Chris Wilkinson, *Supersheds: The Architecture of Long-Span, Large-Volume Buildings* (Oxford: Butterworth, 1991), p. 4.

19 Jonathan Glancey, 'Richard Rogers in Conversation' in *Traces of Peter Rice* (Dublin: The Lilliput Press, 2012), p. 46.

20 Ibid., p. 46.

21 Peter Rice, *An Engineer Imagines* (London: Ellipsis, 1994), p. 29.

22 For more on Hunt's early career, see Nigel Dale, *Connexions: The Unseen Hand of Tony Hunt* (Dunbeath: Whittles, 2012) and Anthony Hunt, *Tony Hunt's Sketchbook* (Oxford: Butterworth-Heinemann, 1999).

23 Interview with Norman Foster, *Building Design*, 12 October 1973, p. 5.

24 Glancey, *Engineering a Thing of Beauty*, p. 17.

25 See C.P. Silver, 'Brunel's Crimean War Hospital – Renkioi Revisited', *Journal of Medical Biography*, November 1998, Vol. 6, Issue 4, pp. 234–9.

26 James Benet, *SCSD: The Project and the Schools, a Report from Educational Facilities Laboratories* (New York: Educational Facilities Labs., Inc., 1967), p. 3.

27 Norman Foster, 'Norman Foster on Technology', *The Architectural Review*, January 2017, in reference to Norman Foster's 'Town Workshop', *The Architectural Review*, November 1969, <https://www.architectural-review.com/ar-120/ar-120-norman-foster-on-technology/10015754.article> [accessed 20 January 2018].

28 Galerie Patrick Seguin, *The Métropole House* (Design Miami/Basel online catalogue, June 2012) <https://www.patrickseguin.com/en/exhibitions/2012/jean-prouve-aluminium-house/> [accessed 23 Feburary 2018].

29 Phillips auction house sold a number of Prouvé demountable structures in 2015, on behalf of Galerie Patrick Seguin. In 2007, hotelier André Balazs purchased one of only three built examples of Prouvé's Maison Tropicale for almost $5 million at auction at Christie's (see *New York Times*, 6 June 2007); he later re-erected the structure for public display outside London's Tate Modern. Recently, Richard Rogers has collaborated with Galerie Patrick Seguin to produce an updated version of the Prouvé House, with additional twenty-first century 'pods' to house updated services.

30 Rice, *An Engineer Imagines*, p. 115.

31 Richard Rogers, 'La Casa di Vetro di Pierre Chareau', *Domus* Magazine, October 1966, p. 8; as cited in Neil Jackson, *The Modern Steel House* (London: Chapman & Hall, 1996), p. 18.

32 Martin Pawley: 'Towards an Unoriginal Architecture' in Jonathan Hughes and Simon Sadler, *Non-Plan: Essays on Freedom, Participation and Change in Modern Architecture and Urbanism* (Oxford and New York: Routledge, 2000), p. 223.

33 See Martin Pawley, 'Technology Transfer' in *The Architectural Review*, September 1987, republished in *Rethinking Technology: a Reader in Architectural Theory*, ed. by William W. Braham and Jonathan A. Hale (Oxford and New York: Routledge, 2007), pp. 280–93.

34 Banham, 'A Clip-On Architecture', 1965.

35 Cited in Beatriz Colomina, *Clip Stamp Fold: The Radical Architecture of Little Magazines, 196X to 197X* (Barcelona: Actar, 2010), p. 94.

36 Letter from Richard Rogers to architect Robin Spence, 28 April 1987; cited in Jackson, *The Modern Steel House*, p. 143.

37 Colin Davies, *The Prefabricated Home* (London: Reaktion Books, 2006), p. 38.

38 Jackson, *The Modern Steel House*, p. 187.

39 Martin Pawley, 'High-Tech Architecture: History vs. The Parasites', *AA Files*, No. 21, Spring 1991, pp. 26–9.

40 Martin Pawley, 'Artists of the Floating World', *The Observer Review*, 21 August 1994, p.4; cited in Jackson, *The Modern Steel House*, p. 185.

41 Quote by Nic Clear, curator of the exhibition, *Jan Kaplický: Drawings*, The Stephen Lawrence Gallery, University of Greenwich in the *RIBA Journal* review, 13 December 2016.

42 Jan Kaplický and David Nixon, quoted in Wilkinson, *Supersheds*, p. 112.

43 Cited in an exhibition review by Jonathan Glancey, 'Sufferin' Satellites: We've Built the Future!', *The Guardian*, 28 April 2008, <https://www.theguardian.com/artanddesign/2008/apr/28/architecture> [accessed 20 January 2018].

44 Interview by Kester Rattenbury with Archigram member, Dennis Crompton, The Archigram Archival Project, University of Westminster, <http://archigram.westminster.ac.uk/magazine.php?id=96> [accessed 23 February 2018].

45 'Editorial', *Archigram* no. 4, quoted in Colomina, *Clip Stamp Fold*, p. 92.

46 For further exploration of this, see *Hippie Modernism: The Struggle for Utopia*, ed. by Andrew Blaufelt (Minneapolis: Walker Arts Center, 2016).

47 Denise Scott-Brown, *Journal of the American Institute of Planners*, July 1968, p. 230, as cited in Reyner Banham, *Megastructure: Urban Futures of the Recent Past* (London: Thames & Hudson, 1976).

48 Esther Da Costa Meyer, 'Drawn Into The Future: Urban Visions by Mario Chiattone and Antonio Sant'Elia' in *Italian Futurism 1909–1944: Reconstructing The Universe* (New York: Guggenheim Museum, 2014), pp. 140–5.

49 Cedric Price and Joan Littlewood, Fun Palace promotional brochure (Montreal: Canadian Centre for Architecture, 1964).

50 Interview quote from Matt Shaw, 'Relive the glory of the 1970 Osaka Expo', *The Architect's Newspaper*, 18 June 2015.

51 Fumihiko Maki, *Investigations in Collective Form* (St. Louis: Washington University School of Architecture, 1964), pp. 8–13.

52 Banham, *Megastructure*, p. 17.

53 Quoted in the documentary film, *Beaubourg: Four Films*, dir. by Denis Postle (Arts Council England/Concord Media, 1980) [on DVD].

54 Banham, *Megastructure*, p. 100.

55 Quoted in *Beaubourg: Four Films*.

56 Hadas Steiner, *Archigram: The Structure of Circulation* (London: Routledge, 2009), pp. 27–8.

57 Glancey, 'Richard Rogers in Conversation', p. 47.

58 Cedric Price and Joan Littlewood, 'A Laboratory of Fun', *New Scientist*, 14 May 1964, pp. 432–3.

59 Reyner Banham, article originally published in *The Architectural Review*, May 1977 and republished as 'Pompidou cannot be conceived as anything other than a monument', *Architectural Review*, 2 March 2012 <https://www.architectural-review.com/buildings/may-1977-pompidou-cannot-be-perceived-as-anything-but-a-monument/8627187.article> [accessed 20 January 2018].

60 Cedric Price, 'Potteries Thinkbelt Report', as published in *New Society*, June 1966.

61 Barry Bergdoll and Peter Christensen, *Home Delivery: Fabricating the Modern Dwelling*, (New York: Museum of Modern Art, 2008), p. 144.

62 Banham, *Megastructure*, p. 217.

63 Joseph Paxton's evidence to The House of Commons Select Committee on Metropolitan Communications, 7 June 1855. 'Parliamentary records from Hansard online', <http://hansard.millbanksystems.com/> [accessed 20 January 2018].

64 Misha Black, 'A Project for the Universal International Exhibition of 1951', concept proposal, RIBA collections (PA357/5).

65 Quoted during a press conference in the *About Anglia* television news item, 'Architect Denys Lasdun talks about his vision for the soon-to-be-built University of East Anglia', broadcast 1963, East Anglia Film Archive, <http://www.eafa.org.uk/catalogue/213000> [accessed 20 January 2018].

66 Jan Kaplický and David Nixon, 'What Does Living in Space Herald for the Future of Architecture?', *The Architectural Review*, July 1984.

67 Jan Kaplický and David Nixon, quoted in Wilkinson, *Supersheds*, p. 112.

68 Sam Jacob, 'High Tech Primitive: The Architecture of Antarctica' in *Ice Lab: New Architecture and Science in Antarctica*, ed. by Sandra Ross, (London: The British Council/Arts Catalyst 2013), <https://www.artscatalyst.org/geographies/antarctica> pp. 54–75 [accessed 20 January 2018].

69 Charles Jencks, 'High-Tech Slides to Organi-Tech', *ANY: Architecture New York*, no. 10, 1995, pp. 44–9.

70 E.g. the Container City modular construction system using shipping containers at Trinity Buoy Wharf (2001) and the Olympic Broadcast Studios (2012); and the Boxpark 'pop-up' shopping malls in Shoreditch and Croydon.

71 For another recent example, see the recent design for a family home by Henning Stummel (a former architect in Norman Foster's office), consisting of six interconnected steel-clad structures, designed with a modular plan for both private and communal spaces – utilising a commercially available, off-the-shelf metal cladding product called GreenCoat.

72 Jan Kaplický and David Nixon, quoted in Wilkinson, *Supersheds*, p. 112.

SIDE-SLIPPING THE SEVENTIES

In a challenging decade,
the Sainsbury Centre
reaffirmed the role of a
truly progressive architecture

Jonathan Glancey

Design work on the Sainsbury Centre began in 1974. The first three months of a year that witnessed the opening of the first British branch of McDonald's and the jailing of the architect John Poulson on charges of corruption were dominated by the Three-Day Week – an emergency measure by Edward Heath's Conservative government to save electricity as stockpiles of coal fell. That year also saw a national overtime ban by miners followed by a strike, the 'Oil Crisis', prompted by an OPEC (Organisation of the Petroleum Exporting Countries) embargo on sales to Europe, and the onset of Britain's first post-war recession.

Inflation that year rose to 17.2 per cent, while to compound a dismal state of economic affairs, the Provisional IRA bombed a coach on the M62, pubs in Guildford and Birmingham, the Palace of Westminster in June and, three days before Christmas, the Prime Minister's London home in Victoria.

While, with hindsight, it is easy to see 1974 as the year that undermined a more or less consensual post-war belief in what had seemed to be the inevitable and beneficial onward and upward march of technological, political and economic progress, things could seem pretty grim at the time. 'Broken Britain' and 'Third World Britain' were phrases bandied about by academics and newspaper leader writers alike.

In the architectural realm, high-rise housing had fallen from grace in the aftermath of the collapse in May 1968 of the prefabricated concrete 21-storey Ronan Point tower block in Canning Town, East London, just two months after the first council residents had moved in. Four years later, the 57-acre Pruitt-Igoe housing project in St Louis, Missouri, designed by Minoru Yamasaki, the architect of the ill-fated twin towers of New York's World Trade Center, was detonated and demolished. While the St Louis tower blocks were well engineered, ineffective management, poor maintenance and a culture of violence within the project led to its hurried demise.

These events in London and St Louis could be seen as highly visible and newsworthy signs of the decline and fall of a Modern architecture that, rooted in the ideals of the Bauhaus, blossomed from the 1920s and spread around the world post-1945. Here, surely, post-Ronan Point and Pruitt-Igoe, was the opportunity for new kinds of building and development, free of the right-angled and functionalist strictures of the Modern Movement. The polemicist and historian Charles Jencks, who made his name with *Modern Movements in Architecture* (1973), a book demonstrating the multiverse of twentieth-century design, rose to the occasion with *The Language of Post-Modern Architecture* (1977). 'Modern architecture', he wrote, 'died in St Louis, Missouri on July 15, 1972, at 3.32pm (or thereabouts).'[1] Long live Post-Modernism.

The idea of a Postmodern architecture had been explored a decade earlier by the Philadelphia architect Robert Venturi. 'I welcome the problems and exploit the uncertainties [of modern experience]', wrote Venturi in his Postmodern manifesto, *Complexity and Contradiction in Architecture* (1966). The second edition was

Ronan Point, London: construction started in 1966; it was demolished in 1968 following partial collapse after a gas explosion.

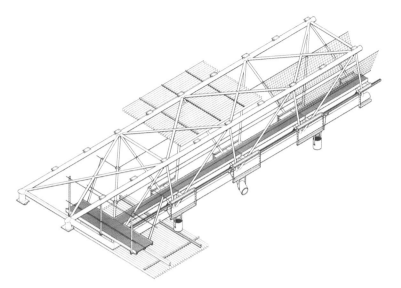

published in 1977. 'I like elements which are hybrid rather than "pure",
compromising rather than "clean" … accommodating rather than
excluding … I am for messy vitality over obvious unity … I prefer
"both-and" to "either-or", black and white, and sometimes gray,
to black or white … An architecture of complexity and contradiction
must embody the difficult unity of inclusion rather than the easy
unity of exclusion.'[2]

In 1966, the sleek corporate architecture of Mies van der Rohe
held sway. While, in Mies's hands, this had much to commend it, in
lesser hands it spelt city streets lined with undistinguished office towers
as if proving the maxim, coined later, 'form follows finance'. Inverting
Mies's maxim 'Less is More', Venturi declared 'Less is a Bore'.

The scene, then, appeared to be set for a playful, expressive
and colourful Postmodern architecture at the very time that Foster
Associates, formed in 1967, designed the Sainsbury Centre. Between
1974 and 1978 on the lakeside fringe of the University of East Anglia,
Foster Associates invented and gave shape to an exquisite and wholly
inclusive silver machine of a building that spoke, without a millimetre's
hesitation, of a logical, benign and singularly beautiful future informed
by the latest in technology, materials, structural engineering and
thinking about what a new-found 'Centre for the Visual Arts' might be.
Side-slipping the insecurities and contradictions of the mid-Seventies,
here was a building that made a confident, technologically inspired
future appear convincingly real.

It offered, too, a convincing riposte to Venturi. Here was a
seductive, glistening building that truly embodied the 'difficult unity
of inclusion rather than the easy unity of exclusion'. In fact, it was the
very process of inclusion – of so many programmatic and functional
elements – that drove the design of the Sainsbury Centre, giving
shape to a building that resolved complexity into a unified and
seamless whole rather than a kaleidoscope of Postmodern fragments.
And it was a building, along with the earlier sheer black glass Willis
Faber & Dumas office headquarters in Ipswich (1970–5), that propelled
Norman Foster into the first rank of contemporary architects.

As impressive as they were, Foster's ascent and the existence
of the Sainsbury Centre were not givens. Both were outside the main
frames of contemporary British architecture and the profession that,
nominally, supported it. 'I was very much an outsider', says Foster,
40 years on. 'It might sound odd to say it, but I still am. I'd long been a
square peg in a round hole, but this had allowed me to look at things
differently, and to question why anything – a building, a machine, an
institution – is as it is.'

Coming to architecture late and from an unusual route – a clerk
in the accountancy department at Manchester Town Hall ('a splendid
building by Alfred Waterhouse … designed through and through'), a
National Service electronics engineer in the RAF, a student making
measured drawings of windmills and barns rather than Beaux-Arts
monuments at the University of Manchester – Foster had little in
common with the majority of young, middle-class British architects.
To a degree, and certainly up to his time as a post-graduate student
at Yale when he met Richard Rogers and was excited to study under
the challenging Paul Rudolph and cosmopolitan Serge Chermayeff,
Foster was self-taught.

As a Manchester schoolboy, he had been thrilled to discover for
himself *Towards a New Architecture*, the 1927 English translation by
Frederick Etchells of Le Corbusier's *Vers une Architecture* (1923) on
the shelves of the Levenshulme Carnegie Library. What most excited
Foster were Le Corbusier's provocative visual juxtapositions, most
memorably the Parthenon facing a multi-winged Caproni Hydroplane.
In the pages of Henry-Russell Hitchcock's *In the Nature of Materials:
1887–1941: The Buildings of Frank Lloyd Wright* (1942), he found a

Above left. Ceiling
structure showing lighting
system and catwalks for
maintenance.

Above. Sunlight casts
patterns across the
perforated louvres lining
the interior.

'more remote fantasy world – science-fiction images of shimmering glass in the Johnson Wax building'. Science fiction itself, from Flash Gordon films to the adventures of the fictional, Manchester-born *Dan Dare, Pilot of the Future* – the lead character of *The Eagle* who flew to the stars from a Frank Lloyd Wright-style Space Fleet headquarters on Morecambe Bay, Lancashire – fuelled Foster's imagination, too.

'As did the pages of the *Architectural Review*', Foster adds, 'which I first saw working in an architect's office – not as an architect – before getting in to Manchester University. I could see that the *AR* was edited by mavericks. I could relate to Jim Richards' series on the Functional Tradition, to Gordon Cullen's Townscape, to Ian Nairn's attacks on Subtopia and to the way a very English tradition was mixed with images and drawings of some of the best new buildings from around the world.'

Le Corbusier was, of course, a maverick, too, an oblique and even puzzling outsider who did much to change the course of twentieth-century architecture. As for his English translator, Frederick Etchells, he was a Vorticist painter who became a Modern architect. The steel-framed, cement-faced office block (1930) he and Herbert Arthur Welch designed in London's High Holborn for the advertising agency W.S. Crawford was perhaps the first truly Modern building of its kind in Britain. And, yet, in 1937 the complex and contradictory Etchells was a founding member, along with John Betjeman, Robert Byron and Osbert Sitwell, of the Georgian Group. Post-war, he worked as a church conservationist and was a devout member of the Society for the Protection of Ancient Buildings.

Foster himself has no difficulty with such talented and complex people. 'I appreciated the inventive buildings of Colonel Seifert, like Centre Point. He tended to be written off by critics at the time, but, with his partner George Marsh, he brought Niemeyer-like excitement into a world of largely dull office buildings.'

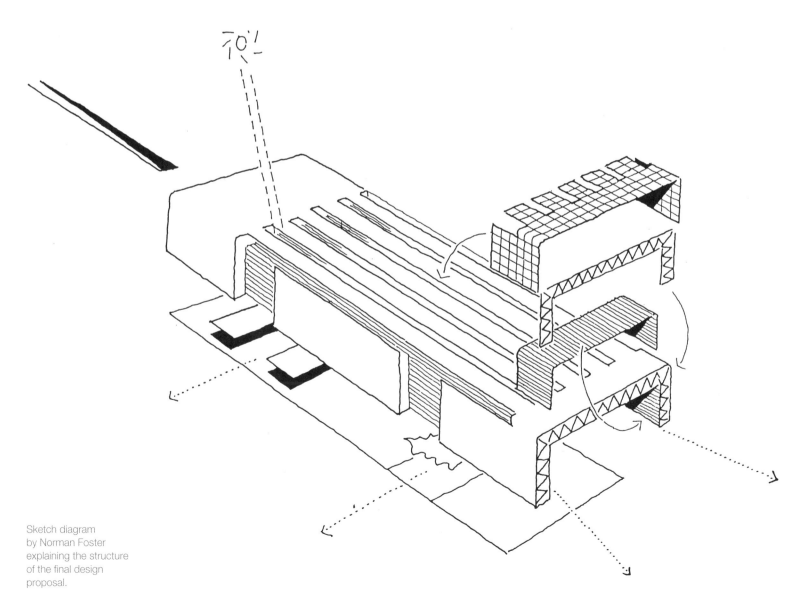

Sketch diagram by Norman Foster explaining the structure of the final design proposal.

Far left. Supermarine Spitfire Mk IX.

Left. The distinctive sliding canopy of the Hawker Hurricane played a key role, as a visual reference, in the design of the 'Cockpit'. Designed by Sidney Camm in 1934, this robust and agile wooden-framed fighter played a key role in the Battle of Britain.

'Mocked in *Private Eye* for continuing to use his army rank "Colonel"', read the *Daily Telegraph*'s obituary of 29 October 2001, 'Seifert was the antithesis of the image of the architect as bohemian artist. His solid businessman-like approach won him few friends in the architectural establishment, which tended to dismiss his work as "development architecture".'[3]

Following their own stars, such mavericks thought for themselves and questioned what they and others knew. 'I'm always looking for mavericks to join us today, just as I did when we were commissioned to design Sainsbury. I like to ask questions. I like to learn. I like to be surprised,' Foster says.

If Foster had been happily surprised by his first sight of Le Corbusier's juxtaposition of the Parthenon and a Caproni Hydroplane, I think he understood the connection subliminally, although this would have been much clearer if Le Corbusier had published his book a decade or so later and shown the streamlined Douglas DC-3 airliner in place of the multi-winged Caproni Hydroplane. I say this because what Foster so admires in the design of modern aircraft is their highly resolved and truly all-inclusive design: 'I loved Concorde. Think of those many complex systems, the sheer number of components worked seamlessly into that highly effective and beautiful shape. Could we do something similar with buildings?'

And, yet, this is very much what the architects, Ictinus and Callicrates working with the sculptor Phidias, had achieved in the design of the Parthenon two-and-a-half thousand years ago. The bare structure we see on the Acropolis today might seem satisfyingly and – in the right light – magnificently simple, and yet, programmatically and culturally, the Parthenon is more complex than any Postmodern building dating from the mid-1970s. The entases of its Doric columns have even been read as symbols of the billowing sails of the Greek warships that allowed Athens to triumph over what had seemed to be the unstoppable might of the vast Persian military machine.

In a neat form of asymmetry, the Sainsbury Centre is easily read as a sublime aircraft hangar, while Foster's delight in the perfectly resolved form of Reginald Mitchell's Supermarine Spitfire turns, too, on the role this magnificent machine played both in reality and in the

imagination in keeping Hitler's formidable war machine on the French side of the English Channel in 1940.

The role aircraft played in the design of Foster buildings from the very beginning with Team 4 (Su Brumwell, Wendy Cheesman, Norman Foster and Richard Rogers, 1963–7) was, in fact, a statement of future intent. Designed for Marcus and Rene Brumwell, the 'Cockpit', for example, was a watertight gazebo close to Creek Vean, the house Team 4 designed for them. Complete with electricity and a small stove, it allowed visitors to look out across Cornwall's Pill Creek – a haven for sailing boats – in all weathers. Rooted in the earth, its superstructure was light and airy. In this sense, it was an early precursor of the Sainsbury Centre. Its profile, says Foster, was adopted from the distinctive sliding canopy of the Hawker Hurricane, the fighter aircraft designed by Sidney Camm that fought alongside Mitchell's Spitfire in the Battle of Britain. Like the Hurricane, its glass canopy roof slid back.

This relationship between the design of aircraft and buildings developed as Foster Associates' projects grew in size and ambition. In 1991, BBC2 invited Foster to choose and celebrate a favourite building for *Building Sights*, a series of fast-paced and insightful mini-documentaries. According to Patrick Uden, producer of Foster's episode, 'After contacting Norman Foster, I decided to offer a new insight into the concept of what a building can be to Ruth Rosenthal, the editor of this weekly 10-minute series. The idea was to capture the dynamics and detail of the magisterial Boeing 747-400 as a piece of architecture, while also revealing how aircraft system building fed into the emerging technology of off-site construction. The commentary, imagery and music are entirely mine, while for Foster it turned out to be a bit of an epiphany moment as he saw his ideas about architecture transformed into a crisp, personal TV polemic.'[4]

Foster's enthusiasm on screen was infectious: 'With about 3,000 square metres of floor space, 15 lavatories, three kitchens and a capacity for up to 367 guests, this is surely a true building … the surprisingly tiny but ruthlessly functional flight deck is a twinkling beauty and the layout is ergonomically efficient. At a more humdrum level, the business-class toilets are admirably space efficient and are finely detailed pieces of industrial architecture. The galleys have a marvellous 'American diner' style … There is a lot to learn from this building. In one sense you could say it is the ultimate technological building site.'[5]

The ergonomic efficiency of the Boeing 747 did indeed play a significant role in the development of the design of the Sainsbury Centre. 'There were many other references', says Foster. 'Paxton's Crystal Palace, the airship hangars at Cardington, Ezra Ehrenkrantz's research into lightweight construction systems in California …'

Foster's exploration of California and its new architecture as a student at Yale was eye-opening, although it showed him more than purely new and inventive designs. It was the liberating, go-to ethos of the country, so very different from a Britain that, often sooty and stuffy, retained ration books after the Second World War until the summer of 1954. 'I came to America over 30 years ago', said Foster giving his Gold Medal address to the AIA (American Institute of Architects) in Washington in 1994. 'America was still the land of my heroes – a very long list – and it still is. I had great expectations and they were fulfilled beyond the dreams I dared not dream … When I came to the United States, I felt I had come home. There was a pride in working and serving. I felt liberated. It is no exaggeration to say that I discovered myself through America.'[6]

Right. Norman Foster on the wing of a Boeing 747-400 (BBC2 *Building Sights*, 1991).

Right. Cross-section through the 'Cockpit' – one sheet from a set of contract drawings drawn by Norman Foster. The materials and finishes specified are simple and direct: exposed concrete, timber framing and glass. This was Team 4's first completed building and the first of a long series of collaborations with Anthony Hunt, who was to be the structural engineer for all Team 4's projects.

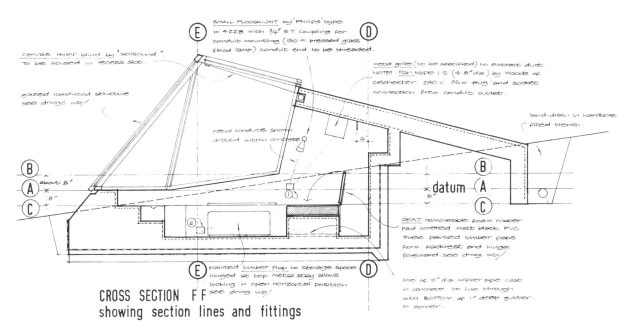

CROSS SECTION FF
showing section lines and fittings

It was, though, a succession of very English projects that triggered Foster's success, while Ezra Ehrenkrantz's research in California was in part rooted in the time he spent at the Building Research Establishment in Hertfordshire, England in the late 1950s, investigating the use of prefabricated light gauge steel frames in building construction. The BRE had played its part, too, in the development of aircraft and weaponry: it was a key player in the lead up to Operation Chastise, the RAF's dam-busting raid of May 1943.

Foster's particular path to architectural practice and his independent interests meant that what he was able to offer clients, as his confidence built, was an approach to building telling new chapters and forming new territories in the story and realm of modern architecture. At the time of the commissioning of the Sainsbury Centre, it was already clear that Foster was beginning to fly in what was to become his own design stratosphere.

An early client, who Foster keeps in touch with, was Fred Olsen, chairman of the Norwegian shipping line founded in 1848. Competing with building contractors rather than rival architects, Norman and Wendy Foster found themselves working up a design for a low-cost 'amenity block' at the company's site in the London Docks at Millwall. Foster played a daring and winning game. He used the competition to question the entire Olsen operation. A new office building with a new entrance for dockers and management alike could occupy an empty firebreak slot between two warehouses or transit sheds. It would include a staff canteen open to everyone. Impressed by Foster's ability to 'ask the right questions', Fred Olsen allowed

the young practice to develop and build a project more-or-less out of thin air.

Writing in *Design* in 1970, Alastair Best, an early champion of Foster Associates, observed, 'It is the reflective glazing of the amenity building – usually connected with the rich executive pastures of Manhattan and Chicago – that is its most unexpected feature. By day the glass, which was made in Pittsburgh to the architects' specification, throws back a rippling image of the dockside scene; by night the picture is reversed and the eye has an uninterrupted view of ground floor canteen and landscaped first floor offices.' He continued, 'Inside colour has been used with an exquisite sensibility – quite unlike the typical killjoy "architect's interior"'. In Best's mind, this added up 'to an environment more in tune with limpwristed aesthetes than with the brawny, matter of fact habitués of the London docks. But the men seem to like it; and so they should, since a ten-man works committee drawn equally from the management and the terminal force met regularly to hammer out the architects' brief … present lack of a licence to sell alcohol in the canteen appears to be upsetting some … but as one superintendent put it, with a philosophical smile, "we can't have everything all at once."'[7]

Here, in the seemingly unlikely setting of the rough and ready London docks – a part of London all but unknown to the English middle classes – Foster had pulled off several quite brilliant tricks at once. Effectively, he had invented his own brief. He had used his knowledge of American construction to source a brand-new heat- and light-reflective glazed curtain wall system that undercut the price of anything remotely close in terms of design and specification available in Britain. He had revolutionised the way dock buildings were seen, while profoundly changing the relationship between workers and management.

The Fred Olsen Amenity Building (1968–9) was rightly admired, winning the attention of future business clients and not least IBM, Willis Faber & Dumas and Sir Robert Sainsbury. In 1983, Sainsbury introduced Norman Foster as RIBA Royal Gold Medallist. 'When Norman accepted the commission', he said, 'there was no written brief – in fact there never was one. Norman's task was to give substance to a somewhat ill-defined concept. We wanted him, in providing a home for our collection, to give members of the University and visitors the opportunity to look at works of art in the natural context of their daily work and life and, above all, to enjoy our collection as we have done. Sensual enjoyment is no bar to the pursuit of knowledge or intellectual understanding. All this called for a place in which people could relax, look at works of art in a leisurely manner if they so wished, work, read a novel or just dream away. Such a place would surely appeal equally to outside scholars and lay members of the public as to men and women in the University. That was Norman's brief … and it was to be developed and elaborated in the course of many, many hours of discussion and travel during the planning stage.'[8]

'It was an exciting, open-ended brief', says Foster. 'We could have proposed a sequence of pavilions housing the main elements – the Sainsbury's art collection donated to the University in 1973, the history of art school, a senior common room, a special exhibitions pavilion and a restaurant – but these elements connected to one another very strongly and we knew we had a case for a single building.

'Robert and Lisa's collection, though, was very varied. I remember first going to see them in Smith Square [Westminster] and being delighted by finding a Henry Moore [*Mother and Child*] at the bottom of the stair, a Giacometti sculpture [*Standing Woman*] in the living room, a Francis Bacon portrait of Lady Sainsbury over the fireplace, African masks in Sir Robert's study and bedroom and any number of tiny carvings. They were keen to stress that all these works could be displayed in a space of uniform height. We came round to the idea of a building that was, in effect, a single volume.'

Early design drawings and models, however, soon proved that a large single volume, no matter how appealing as a concept – not least because a tall space would belie the need for costly air-conditioning – would become messy once kitchens, lavatories, dark rooms for photography, mechanical equipment and other building services were added. Gradually, a solution emerged. The building,

Opposite. Fred Olsen
Amenity Building
Millwall Docks,
London, 1968–70
Photographed at night.

Right. Sketch by
Norman Foster: the
architect's Caproni
sailplane
soars over the
Sainsbury Centre.

engineered by Anthony Hunt, would be double-skinned, much like an airliner. The gap between the inner frame of the building and its outer skin would, at 8 feet (2.44 metres), be wide enough to accommodate ancillary spaces and functions, including a system of mechanically operated louvres controlling the amount of daylight entering through the rooflight panels. Lightweight catwalks in the roof space existed solely to allow servicing of lighting and louvres.

The net effect was a beautiful, diaphanous space, its character changing with the ever-morphing Norfolk light. As Graham Vickers, a design critic, wrote when the building was new, 'The louvres become translucent, celebrating the openness and lightness of the trusses and allowing views up through the length of the roof. The effect is one of remarkable finesse, the layers of louvre, truss structure, catwalk grille and balustrade combining to create weightless architectural abstractions, constantly changing and suffused by daylight.'[9]

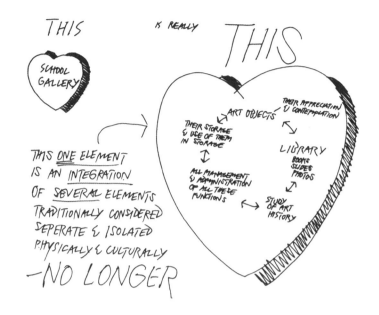

Even then, critics have tended to see what they wanted to see. For Charles Jencks, 'All activities [inside the Sainsbury Centre] are banished to the perimeter or dwarfed behind partitions as the universal space of Mies van der Rohe reigns triumphant over time, function and locale.'[10] No Mies space, however, is quite like this. In terms of its form and construction, the Sainsbury Centre is more Boeing than Bauhaus, while the light that diffuses through its roof panels, through its mesmerising pattern of sun louvres, is the light that haunts the paintings of the Norwich painters John Crome and John Sell Cotman. In a county of large agricultural buildings, of airbases and aircraft hangars, the Sainsbury Centre feels at home.

As Peter Cook noted in his criticism of the Sainsbury Centre in the October 1978 issue of the AR, 'There is an airy green haze reflected on the ceiling, its source hidden. The haze must surely be created by a strong light source beaming back from a highly pigmented carpet. But no, its source is that of the trees outside, framed and captured by the enormous [glazed] end of the box. And such is our elation, that the trees themselves can surely only be a superb, animated photomural'.[11]

Again, the Sainsbury Centre was not altogether some *deus ex machina*, some Buckminster Fuller-inspired Spaceship Earth landed on the hem of the University of East Anglia. In its own particular way, it belongs to its surroundings, while subtly challenging the architectural status quo. As Suzanne Stephens wrote in *Progressive Architecture* in February 1979, 'The Sainsbury Centre's design is shown to best effect in a rural setting rather than an urban one, for its sensitive siting means

Above left. Lisa and Robert Sainsbury at home in Smith Square, London, with a 1920s bronze cast of *The Little Dancer Aged Fourteen* by Edgar Degas, now in the Sainsbury Centre.

Left. The Sainsburys with Norman Foster at the opening of The Crescent Wing, Sainsbury Centre, 1991.

Above: Norman Foster's sketch of an all-embracing centre for visual arts to be housed in a single structure (1974).

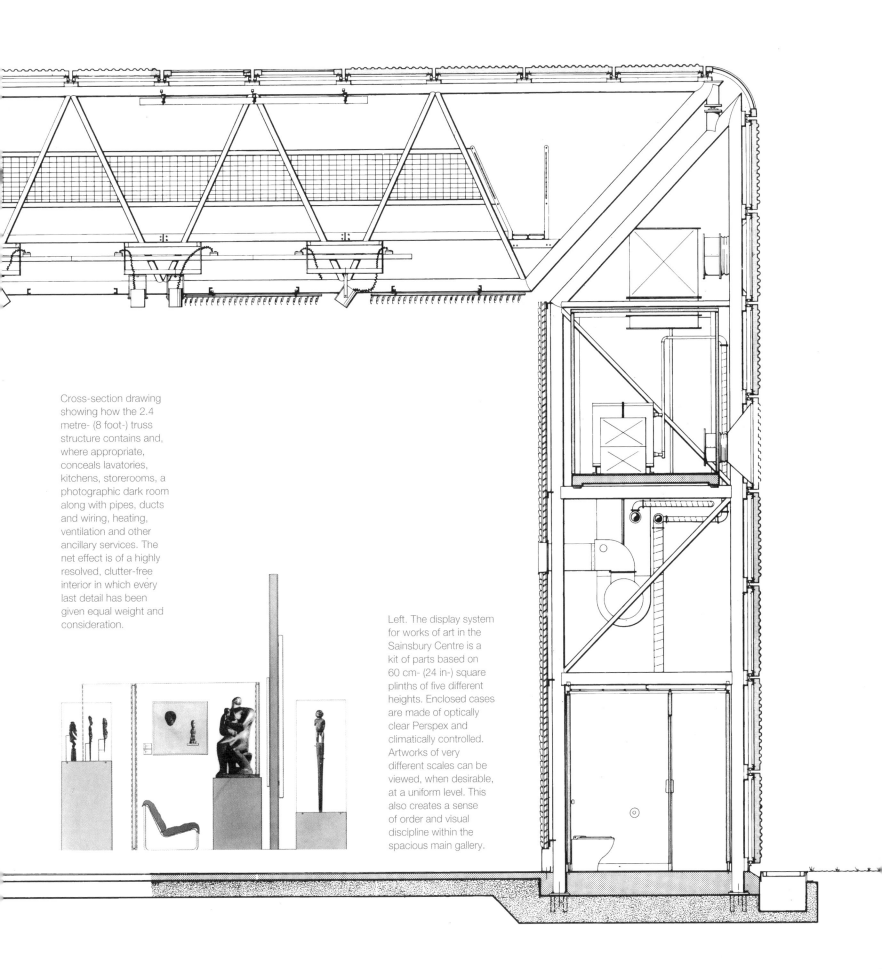

Cross-section drawing showing how the 2.4 metre- (8 foot-) truss structure contains and, where appropriate, conceals lavatories, kitchens, storerooms, a photographic dark room along with pipes, ducts and wiring, heating, ventilation and other ancillary services. The net effect is of a highly resolved, clutter-free interior in which every last detail has been given equal weight and consideration.

Left. The display system for works of art in the Sainsbury Centre is a kit of parts based on 60 cm- (24 in-) square plinths of five different heights. Enclosed cases are made of optically clear Perspex and climatically controlled. Artworks of very different scales can be viewed, when desirable, at a uniform level. This also creates a sense of order and visual discipline within the spacious main gallery.

that the building opens out to views of the natural landscape … In the pastoral milieu, this kind of form – minimal, lightweight, reflective and almost transparent from one end to the other – intrudes only reticently on the landscape. Little more could be asked of it, except for it to be pushed to its logical conclusion and become virtually invisible.'[12]

From 1966, Norfolk was home to Lotus Engineering, the sports and racing car company founded by Colin Chapman and Colin Dare, and newly established at the former RAF Hethel near Wymondham, an airbase seven miles from Norwich used extensively by the USAF during World War Two. Admired by Foster, Lotus cars were designed, to a forensic degree, to be as light as possible. Lithe machines like the original Lotus Elite and Lotus Elan are perfect visual foils to the lightweight Foster building.

The structure of the Sainsbury Centre, with panels mounted on steel trusses also calls to mind the *superleggera* (super-lightweight) form of construction patented by Felice Bianchi Anderloni for Carrozzeria Touring, Milan, in 1936. Small-diameter steel tubes were covered by lightweight aluminium panels attached at their edges, a characteristic of such charismatic cars as the Alfa Romeo 8C 2900 Mille Miglia (1936), BMW 328 (1936), Maserati 3500GT (1957) and the Aston-Martin DB4 (1958) and DB5 (1963).

Opposite. The restaurant, for visitors and employees, is located at the western end of the building. It looks out over the landscape through the huge full-height window.

Above. The roof grid is designed to balance artificial and ever-changing natural lighting. Spotlights highlight particular objects and displays, while ultraviolet light is filtered out to protect artworks.

Below. 'How much does your building weigh, Mr Foster?' A very modest 5,916 tons. Buckminster Fuller (right) and Foster meet at the Sainsbury Centre in 1978.

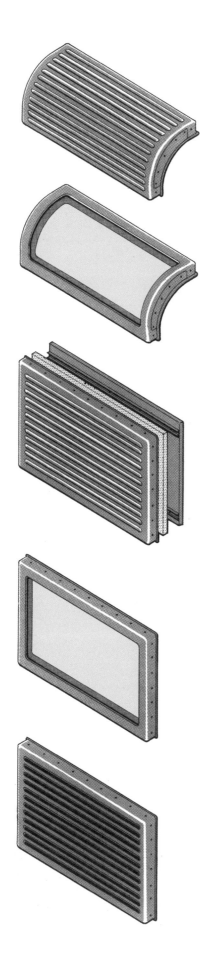

Unlike Foster's favoured *Architectural Review*, *Architectural Design (AD)* magazine was a hotbed of sometimes abstruse architectural theory: 'The excitement and contention that has been aroused by the Sainsbury Centre suggests that it is indeed a polemical work of architecture.'[13] While Foster might well demur, the August 1978 issue of *AD* went further still. According to the – evidently aroused – architect and academic Doug Clelland, 'The building should be understood for what it is – a fetishist expression. Like the sexual fetish of leather, this building celebrates the cladding of the object – the aluminium trappings, clips, straps and other paraphernalia … Yet what a trivial and peripheral business is all that.'[14]

If the Sainsbury Centre was in any way fetishist and sexualised, then the same, presumably, is true of Reginald Mitchell's Spitfire (1936), Malcolm Sayer's Le Mans-conquering D-Type Jaguar (1954), Sir Nigel Gresley's record-breaking streamlined A4 express passenger steam locomotives (1935) for the London and North Eastern Railway and, perhaps, Mies's Tugendhat House (1930). As Robert Sainsbury observed wryly, 'It is certainly true that Norman's building has aroused extraordinary passions among architects, writers and art historians. My personal prize goes to the description of the building as "fetishist expressionism"'.[15]

'What was really exciting', says Foster, 'is Sir Robert and Lady Sainsbury's willingness to allow the building to become whatever it needed to be. They were the ideal clients, questioning yet hugely

Drawings of details of the original external cladding system. The original cladding system consisted of panels of sandwich construction, with a pressed outer skin of anodised aluminium and a core of 100 mm (4 in) Phenolux foam, which gave a very high insulation value.

Opposite. A building survey undertaken in 1988 showed that the original cladding panels had deteriorated and needed replacing. A chemical reaction had set in between the phenolic foam insulation of the panels and their superplastic alloy skins. The replacement panels were smooth and white, giving the building a fresh and even sleeker look than before, and framed in the same material as the glazing.

Above. Superplastic aluminium cladding panels for the Sainsbury Centre.

Left. The ribbed panelling of the Citroën 2CV van.

supportive. They were like second parents to me.' In other ways, their support was unquestioning. When in the late 1980s, the panels of the building degraded because of an unexpected and destructive chemical reaction between insulating phenolic foam inside the panels and the superplastic alloy of their outer shells, these were replaced with higher specification panels, and that was that. The bill was not discussed in public, but was met by a grant from the Sainsbury family foundation.

This turn of events raised the issue of change. If it is possible to upgrade a building over time, how should this be done? In the case of the Sainsbury Centre, the new flat white panels that replaced the original corrugated Citröen van-style panels changed the appearance of the building. 'Change, though', says Foster, 'is the only constant'. Although large numbers of railway enthusiasts quibbled, for example, with upgrades made to Gresley's LNER A3 Pacifics, among them *Flying Scotsman*, from the late 1950s, these locomotives entered their fourth decade in service on the East Coast mainline more than capable of maintaining accelerated express passenger timetables prompted by dieselisation.

Equally, under the direction of Supermarine's chief designer Joseph Smith, the Spitfire was constantly updated between the Battle of Britain and for some years after the fall of the Axis powers in 1945. Reginald Mitchell, who designed the prototype and Mk I production Spitfire, and who had died in 1937, would have insisted on doing the same thing. Why should a building, designed for change, be any different? Trains, planes and cars are design references Foster is fond of quoting.

During construction of the Sainsbury Centre – and despite the rise of Postmodernism alongside Punk, and a fashion for bricky, tweedy British buildings (a riposte to concrete) – evidence of a modern world in tune with the ideals and aesthetic of the Sainsbury Centre emerged in the guise of trains, planes and personal technology. British Rail's HST (High Speed Train), styled by Kenneth Grange, was a world leader when launched in 1976. Here was a streamlined train capable of cruising at a sustained 125mph. It is still very much in service today. Concorde began service with British Airways that year.

Right. Mezzanine and exhibition space with dividers to change the layout of the room.

Opposite. The vehicle delivery ramp emerges from the building's west end, but by using the natural contours of the land and the cover of trees for camouflage, it remains invisible from the building itself. Concealed underground, the loading bays are provided with the best possible security.

In 1978, as inventive new talents like Bruce Springsteen, Elvis Costello, Blondie and Kraftwerk revolutionised the music charts, British Aerospace revealed its formidable, hi-tech Sea Harrier as McDonnell Douglas showed off the paces of the AV-8B Harrier II Jump Jet with its single carbon-fibre wing. Grand Prix racing was dominated that year by the Lotus 79, the first Formula One car to take full advantage of ground effect aerodynamics. The least 'bricky' or 'tweedy' of cars, it was also extremely light due to its aluminium honeycomb construction. As for mobile phones, personal stereos and hand-held computers, these were waiting impatiently in the wings, bleeping and winking. The world of stratospheric technology posited by Foster from the late 1960s and expressed so clearly in the architectural lineaments of the Sainsbury Centre was about to become the mainstream rather than the slipstream.

Not that Britain was quite out of the soot, smoke and smog of the post-war era. As if to drive home the point, a year after the opening of the Sainsbury Centre and underlining the country's reliance on coal, ten miners died in a methane gas explosion at Golbourne Colliery near Wigan.

'As for the Sainsbury Centre, it had been touch and go', says Foster. 'We were a small team then and there was no guarantee that we would make it. Wendy and I thought very seriously about moving to the US, imagining we would be more at home, more accepted there.' But, with the exquisite silver machine they landed on the fringe of the University of East Anglia campus between 1974 and 1978, the Fosters had extruded their own gold.

Much of this essay is based on an interview with Norman Foster on 29 January 2018. All other sources are noted below.

Notes

1 Charles Jencks, *The Language of Post-Modern Architecture* (London 1977).
2 Robert Venturi, *Complexity and Contradiction in Architecture* (New York: The Museum of Modern Art, 1966).
3 *Daily Telegraph*, 29 October 2001.
4 Patrick Uden www.uden.com (site currently under construction).
5 *Building Sights*, dir. by Patrick Uden, BBC2, Series 3: 1 *Boeing 747*, first broadcast 15 January 1991.
6 Norman Foster, AIA Gold Medal speech, Washington DC, 1 February 1994.
7 Alastair Best, *Design*, May 1970, pp. 23–30.
8 Sir Robert Sainsbury, RIBA Gold Medal presentation, London, 21 June 1983.
9 *Norman Foster, Works 1*, ed. by David Jenkins (London, Munich and New York: Prestel, 2002).
10 Charles Jencks, *Current Architecture* (London 1982).
11 Peter Cook, *Architectural Review*, November 1978.
12 Suzanne Stephens, *Progressive Architecture*, February 1979.
13 Editorial, *AD Profile* 19, August 1978.
14 Doug Clelland, *AD Profile* 19, August 1978.
15. Sir Robert Sainsbury, London, 21 June 1983.

UNDER CONSTRUCTION: BUILDING THE SAINSBURY CENTRE

NO ENTRY
TO UNAUTHORISED PERSONS
VEHICULAR ACCESS TO FOOD
RESEARCH INSTITUTE ONLY
WEIGHT LIMIT : 2 TON/AXLE
4 TON VEHICLE

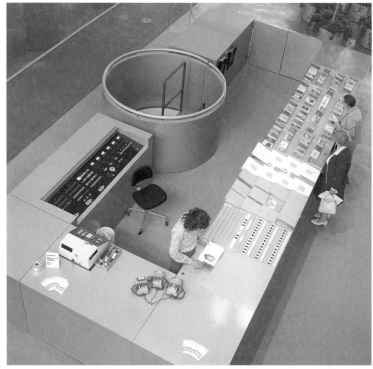

Bibliography

'Architect Denys Lasdun talks about his vision for the soon-to-be-built University of East Anglia', *About Anglia*, Anglia Television, 1963, East Anglia Film Archive, <http://www.eafa.org.uk/catalogue/213000> [accessed 20 January 2018]

Banham, Reyner, *Theory and Design in the First Machine Age* (London: The Architectural Press, 1960)

Banham, Reyner, 'A Clip-On Architecture', *Design Quarterly* No. 63, 1965

Banham, Reyner, *Megastructure: Urban Futures of the Recent Past* (Thames & Hudson, London, 1976)

Banham, Reyner, article originally published in *The Architectural Review*, May 1977 and republished as 'Pompidou cannot be conceived as anything other than a monument', *Architectural Review*, 2 March 2012 <https://www.architectural-review.com/buildings/may-1977-pompidou-cannot-be-perceived-as-anything-but-a-monument/8627187.article> [accessed 20 January 2018]

Barry, Kevin, ed., *Traces of Peter Rice* (Dublin: The Lilliput Press, 2012)

Benet, James, *SCSD: The Project and the Schools, a Report from Educational Facilities Laboratories* (New York: Educational Facilities Labs., Inc., 1967)

Bergdoll, Barry and Christensen, Peter, *Home Delivery: Fabricating the Modern Dwelling* (New York: Museum of Modern Art, 2008)

Best, Alastair, 'Just arrived in port: a new deal for the dockers', *Design*, May 1970, pp. 23–30

Blaufelt, Andrew, ed., *Hippie Modernism: The Struggle for Utopia* (Minneapolis: Walker Arts Center, 2016)

Buchanan, Peter, 'High-Tech: Another British Thoroughbred', *The Architectural Review*, Issue 174, 1983, pp. 15–19

Clelland, Doug, *AD Profile 19*, August 1978

Colomina, Beatriz, *Clip Stamp Fold: The Radical Architecture of Little Magazines*, 196X to 197X (Barcelona: Actar, 2010)

Cook, Peter, ed., *Archigram* (New York: Praeger, 1973)

Cook, Peter, 'Sainsbury Centre for the Visual Arts Criticism', *Architectural Review*, November 1978, pp. 335–6

Da Costa Meyer, Esther, 'Drawn Into The Future: Urban Visions by Mario Chiattone and Antonio Sant'Elia' in *Italian Futurism 1909–1944: Reconstructing The Universe* (New York: Guggenheim Museum, 2014) pp. 140–5

Dale, Nigel, *Connexions: The Unseen Hand of Tony Hunt* (Dunbeath: Whittles, 2012)

Davies, Colin, *High Tech Architecture* (London: Thames & Hudson, 1988)

Davies, Colin, *The Prefabricated Home* (London: Reaktion Books, 2006)

'Editorial', *AD Profile 19*, August 1978

Foster, Norman, AIA Gold Medal speech, Washington DC, 1 February 1994

Foster, Norman, 'Norman Foster on Technology', *Architectural Review*, 5 January 2017, <https://www.architectural-review.com/ar-120/ar-120-norman-foster-on-technology/10015754.article> [accessed 20 January 2018]

Fraser, Murray with Kerr, Joe, *Architecture and the 'Special Relationship': The American Influence on Post-War British Architecture* (Oxford and New York: Routledge, 2007)

Gannon, Todd, *Reyner Banham and the Paradoxes of High Tech* (Los Angeles: The Getty Research Centre, 2017)

Grimshaw, Nicholas, dir., 'Service Tower for Student Housing', <https://grimshaw.global/projects/service-tower-for-student-housing/> [accessed 14 February 2018]

Glancey, Jonathan, 'Engineering a Thing of Beauty', *The Independent*, 23 January 1991, p. 17

Glancey, Jonathan, 'Sufferin' Satellites: We've Built the Future!', *The Guardian*, 28 April 2008, <https://www.theguardian.com/artanddesign/2008/apr/28/architecture> [accessed 20 January 2018]

Harris, James and Pui-K Li, Kevin, *Masted Structures in Architecture* (Oxford: Butterworth, 1996)

Hunt, Anthony, *Tony Hunt's Sketchbook* (Oxford: Butterworth-Heinemann, 1999)

'Interview with Norman Foster', *Building Design*, 12 October 1973, p. 5

Jackson, Neil, *The Modern Steel House* (London: Chapman & Hall, 1996)

Jacob, Sam, 'High Tech Primitive: The Architecture of Antarctica' in *Ice Lab: New Architecture and Science in Antarctica*, ed. by Sandra Ross, (London: The British Council/Arts Catalyst, 2013), <https://www.artscatalyst.org/geographies/antarctica> pp. 54–75 [accessed 20 January 2018]

'Jan Kaplický: Drawings', review in *RIBA Journal*, 13 December 2016

Jencks, Charles, *The Language of Post-Modern Architecture* (London: Academy Editions, 1977)

Jencks, Charles, 'Postmodern vs Late-Modern' in *Zeitgeist in Babel: The Postmodernist Controversy*, ed. by Ingeborg Hoesterey (Bloomington and Indianapolis: Indiana University Press, 1991) pp. 4–21

Jencks, Charles and Chaitkin, William, *Current Architecture* (London: Academy Editions, 1982)

Jencks, Charles and Silver, Nathan, *Adhocism: The Case for Improvisation* (London: Secker and Warburg, 1972; republished Cambridge, MA: MIT Press, 2013)

Jencks, Charles, 'High-Tech Slides to Organi-Tech', *ANY: Architecture New York*, no. 10, 1995, pp. 44–9

Jenkins, David, ed., with Norman Foster, *On Foster … Foster On* (Munich, London and New York: Prestel, 2000)

Jenkins, David, ed., *Norman Foster: Works 1* (London, Munich and New York: Prestel, 2002)

Kaplický, Jan and Nixon, David, 'What Does Living in Space Herald for the Future of Architecture?', *The Architectural Review*, July 1984

Kron, Joan and Slesin, Suzanne, *High Tech: The Industrial Style and Source Book for the Home* (New York: C.N. Potter, 1978)

Maki, Fumihiko, *Investigations in Collective Form* (St. Louis: Washington University School of Architecture, 1964), pp. 8–13

Pawley, Martin, 'High-Tech Architecture: History vs. The Parasites', *AA Files*, No. 21, Spring 1991, pp. 26–9

Pawley, Martin, 'Artists of the Floating World', *The Observer Review*, 21 August 1994, p. 4

Pawley, Martin, 'Towards an Unoriginal Architecture' in Jonathan Hughes and Simon Sadler, *Non-Plan: Essays on Freedom, Participation and Change in Modern Architecture and Urbanism* (Oxford and New York: Routledge, 2000) p. 222–31

Pawley, Martin, 'Technology Transfer' in *The Architectural Review*, September 1987, republished in *Rethinking Technology: a Reader in Architectural Theory*, ed. by William W. Braham and Jonathan A. Hale (Oxford and New York: Routledge, 2007), pp. 280–93

Postle, Denis, dir., *Beaubourg: Four Films*, (Arts Council England/Concord Media, 1980) [on DVD]

Powell, Kenneth, *Richard Rogers: Complete Works Volume 1* (London: Phaidon, 1999)

Price, Cedric and Littlewood, Joan, 'A Laboratory of Fun', *New Scientist*, 14 May 1964, pp. 432–3

Price, Cedric, 'Potteries Thinkbelt Report', *New Society*, June 1966

Rattenbury, Kester with Crompton, Dennis, 'The Archigram Archival Project', University of Westminster, <http://archigram.westminster.ac.uk/magazine.php?id=96> [accessed 23 February 2018]

Rice, Peter, *An Engineer Imagines* (London: Ellipsis, 1994)

'Richard Seifert', *Daily Telegraph*, 29 October 2001, <https://www.telegraph.co.uk/news/obituaries/1360803/Richard-Seifert.html> [accessed 5 Feburary 2018]

Rogers, Richard, 'La Casa di Vetro di Pierre Chareau', *Domus* Magazine, October 1966, p. 8

Sadler, Simon, 'L'Architecture dans le Salon: The Civic Architecture of a Projective Modernism' in *Neo-avant-garde and Postmodern: Postwar Architecture in Britain and Beyond* (Studies in British Art 21), ed. by Mark Crinson and Claire Zimmerman (New Haven and London: Yale, 2010), pp. 367–85

Sainsbury, Sir Robert, introducing Norman Foster as RIBA Royal Gold Medallist, London, 21 June 1983

Shaw, Matt, 'Relive the glory of the 1970 Osaka Expo', *The Architect's Newspaper*, 18 June 2015, <https://archpaper.com/2015/06/relive-glory-1970-osaka-expo-complete-space-frames-metabolism-inflatables-geodesic-domes/> [accessed 20 January 2018]

Silver, C.P., 'Brunel's Crimean War Hospital – Renkioi Revisited' in *Journal of Medical Biography*, November 1998, Vol. 6, Issue 4, pp. 234–9

The Métropole House (Design Miami/Basel online catalogue, Galerie Patrick Seguin, June 2012), <https://www.patrickseguin.com/en/exhibitions/2012/jean-prouve-aluminium-house/> [accessed 23 Feburary 2018]

Steiner, Hadas, *Archigram: The Structure of Circulation* (London: Routledge, 2009)

Stephens, Suzanne, *Progressive Architecture*, February 1979

Rybczynski, Witold, *The Biography of a Building: How Robert Sainsbury and Norman Foster Built a Great Museum* (London: Thames & Hudson, 2011)

Uden, Patrick (dir.), 'Boeing 747', *Building Sights*, BBC2, Series 3: 1, first broadcast 15 January 1991

Venturi, Robert, *Complexity and Contradiction in Architecture* (New York: The Museum of Modern Art, 1966)

Wachsmann, Konrad, *The Turning Point of Building: Structure and Design* (New York: Reinhold Publishing Corporation, 1961)

Wilkinson, Chris, *Supersheds: The Architecture of Long-Span, Large-Volume Buildings* (Oxford: Butterworth, 1991)

Acknowledgements

The Sainsbury Centre for Visual Arts would like to thank the following for their support in the planning and staging of the exhibition *SUPERSTRUCTURES: The New Architecture, 1960–1990* and the preparation of this book, published to mark the fortieth anniversary of the Sainsbury Centre.

All lenders to the exhibition have been generous with their time, not only in the loan and preparation of objects, but also in their advice and support with the research process. The Sainsbury Centre wishes to express sincere thanks to the following lenders: Canadian Centre for Architecture; Centre Pompidou, National Museum of Modern Art – Centre for Industrial Creation, Paris; Foster + Partners; Galerie Patrick Seguin; Grimshaw; Hopkins Architects; Ian Ritchie Architects; The National Archives; Norman Foster Foundation; Plus One Gallery; Professor Rodney Kinsman; Rogers Stirk Harbour + Partners; Royal Commission for the Exhibition of 1851; Royal Institute of British Architects; Southampton City Art Gallery; the Victoria and Albert Museum and all private lenders.

A huge thanks to Dr Nicholas Warr, Curator of Photographic Collections in the Department of Art History and World Art Studies at the University of East Anglia, for his infinite kindness and dedication in selecting many of the images that constitute the photo essay in this book.

We also express our thanks to the sponsors of the exhibition: Litestructures; Hudson & Partners, Willis Towers Watson and Loveday and Partners.

In addition, we gratefully acknowledge the following individuals for their support in the development of the project: Norman Foster, Katy Harris and Gayle Mault (Foster + Partners); Gabriel Hernández, Margarita Suárez and Alba Suárez (The Norman Foster Foundation); Vicki MacGregor and Heather Puttock (Rogers Stirk Harbour + Partners); Jack Holdsworth, Chris Spence and Andrew Whalley (Grimshaw); Michael and Patty Hopkins, Hannah Dickenson and Jenny Stevens (Hopkins Architects); Ian Ritchie; Lucy Keohane (Patrick Seguin); Professor Rodney Kinsman and Alice Volpi (OMK); Angela Kenny (Royal Commission for the Exhibition of 1851); Ben and Sheila Johnson; Julius Bryant, Olivia Horsfall-Turner and Christopher Wilk (Victoria and Albert Museum); Catriona Cornelius, Charles Hind and Fiona Orsini (RIBA Library Drawings and Archives Collections); Caroline Camus and Jean-Claude Boulet (Centre Pompidou); Ishwant Sahota and Kate Narewska (The National Archives); Dan Matthews, Steve Marshall and Clare Mitchell (Southampton City Art Gallery); Maggie Bollaert and Colin Pettit (Plus One Gallery); Patricia Hewitt; Pete Huggins; Jonathan Glancey; Nathan Silver; Tim Abrahams; Adrian Forty; Otto Saumarez Smith; Emma Westbrandt (Horden Cherry Lee Architects); Claire Curtice (Hugh Broughton Architects); David Noble; James Mortimer; Richard Davies; Carl Fischer; Eamonn O'Mahony; Andy Crouch; Keith Hunter; Timo Huber; Gianni Berengo Gardin; Dave Bower; Paul Harmer; Tim Street-Porter.

The curators (Jane Pavitt and Abraham Thomas) would like to extend their heartfelt thanks to the following people for making the exhibition and book possible. Our first thanks go to Monserrat Pis Marcos, the project curator, who worked tirelessly and enthusiastically to bring this project to fruition, keeping us on our toes and to a tight timetable. It would not have been possible without her. To Andrés Ros Soto, the exhibition designer, and Andrew Johnson, the designer of the book and exhibition graphics, for their creativity, ingenuity and enthusiasm for the subject matter. To George Sexton Associates, the exhibition lighting designers. To Rachel Giles, for her editorial work on the book. To Carrie Rees and her team (Rees & Co) for publicity work. To Ghislaine Wood (whose idea this was), Paul Greenhalgh and Calvin Winner (Sainsbury Centre) for commissioning the project and providing expert counsel. To all the staff team at the Sainsbury Centre who contributed in various ways. To Kingston School of Art (Kingston University London) and its Modern Interiors Research Centre, who supported Jane Pavitt's time on the research project and were also co-organisers of the conference. To the Renwick Gallery, Smithsonian Institution, who supported Abraham Thomas' time. We would also like to thank our families for their patience and support.

The Sainsbury Centre would not exist without the extraordinary generosity of Robert and Lisa Sainsbury, who not only gave their collection but the building that houses it. This book is dedicated to them, and to all those involved in the making of this remarkable superstructure – the architects, engineers, designers, consultants, technicians, construction workers and employees who brought the project to fruition forty years ago, as well as those who have contributed to its care and upkeep ever since.

Photographic Credits

Arcaid Images/Alamy Stock Photo: 20 (right)

Architectural Press Archive/RIBA Collections: 29, 40 (top), 41

Art History Photographic Collection. Sainsbury Centre for Visual Arts. Photograph by Michael Brandon-Jones: 10–11, 54–5, 74 (all images), 75, 85, 89 (bottom)

Art History Photographic Collection. Sainsbury Centre for Visual Arts. Photograph by Stella Shackle: 5, 72–3, 90 (all images), 91 (all images), 92, 93 (all images)

BBC Photo Library: 61 (bottom)

Otto Baitz/Esto: 47 (top)

John Batchelor/Foster + Partners: 37 (left)

Dave Bower: 28

Richard Bryant/Arcaid Images, courtesy of Rogers Stirk Harbour + Partners: 48

Canadian Centre for Architecture © Arata Isozaki: 40 (top right)

Peter Cook/VIEW: 51 (bottom)

Andy Crouch: 45 (bottom)

Richard Davies: 14 (right), 30 (bottom), 68 (middle))

ESA/Foster + Partners: 52

Originally published in *Esquire* Magazine © Carl Fischer: 20 (left)

Flickr: heyday44, 24 (left); Steve Cadman, 35 (bottom); Derek Voller, 57

Norman Foster: 18, 22

Courtesy of the Norman Foster Foundation: 2, 6, 8 (both images), 59, 63, 64, 76, 77, 80 (all images), 81, 86, 87, 88, 89 (top left) , 94, 95, 96 (all images), 97, 98, 99, 100, 101, 102 (all images), 103

Foster + Partners: 16, 61 (bottom), 65 (all images), 78–79, 82 (all images), 83 (all images), 84, 89 (top right), 104–105

Foster + Partners/Ken Kirkwood: 71, 106, 107, 108, 109

J. Paul Getty Trust. Getty Research Institute, Los Angeles (2004.R.10): 33, 34

Grimshaw: 23 (right)

Halley VI British Antarctic Station designed by Hugh Broughton Architects and AECOM for British Antarctic Survey. Photo: © James Morris: 51

Ron Herron Archive. All Rights Reserved, DACS/Artimage 2018: 39

Hopkins Architects: 30 (top)

Designed by Richard Horden Associates, now Horden Cherry Lee Architects: 35 (top)

Hufton + Crow: 50 (left)

Pete Huggins: 19

Keith Hunter: 50 (right)

Jan Kaplický: 58 (left), 68 (left)

Ken Kirkwood: 17, 46 (bottom), 66, 67 (bottom)

Ken Kirkwood, courtesy of Rogers Stirk Harbour + Partners: 47 (bottom)

Ian Lambot: 49

Library of Congress Prints and Photographs Division Washington, D.C.: 35 (middle)

Library of Congress Prints and Photographs Division Washington, D.C. The Paul Rudolph Archive: 45 (top)

Leipziger Messe: 26

James Mortimer: 15 (bottom)

David Noble, courtesy of Rogers Stirk Harbour + Partners: 15 (top)

Cedric Price fonds, Canadian Centre for Architecture: 40 (bottom), 43

Private Collection: 37 (top right)

RIBA Collections: 27

Rogers Stirk Harbour + Partners. Eamonn O'Mahony: 23 (left)

Sainsbury Centre for Visual Arts, University of East Anglia: 64 (left and bottom left)

School of Art History, University of East Anglia: 14 (left)

Courtesy Galerie Patrick Seguin. © ADAGP, Paris and DACS, London 2018: 31 (top)

Courtesy of Nathan Silver: 37 (bottom right)

Ezra Stoller/Esto: 21 (both images)

Tim Street-Porter: 62

Victoria and Albert Museum, London: 24 (right), 44

Wikimedia Commons: Ralph Roletschek, 18 (botttom); 25; subrealistsandu, 31 (bottom); Brian Minkoff-London Pixels, 36; 38; Jordy Meow, 42 (right); Pseudopanax at English Wikipedia, 60 (left); Adrian Pingstone, 60 (right); Tomeq183, 68 (bottom)

Nigel Young/Foster + Partners: 12, 46 (top), 56, 58 (right), 67 (top), 69 (all images), 70

ZÜND-UP (Timo Huber, W.M. Pühringer, Hermann Simböck, Bertram Mayer). Image courtesy of Timo Huber: 42 (top)